The Art of Becoming An Entrepreneur

The Art Of
Becoming An Entrepreneur

by
Lawrence C. Hagerty

The Art of Becoming An Entrepreneur

2nd Paperback Edition 2015

eBook Edition Published 2011

1st Paperback Edition 1985

About the author: www.LorenzoHagerty.com

Other books by Lorenzo Hagerty

The Chronicles of Lorenzo - Volumes 1 & 2

The Spirit of the Internet

The Genesis Generation

The Milk Punch Regatta & Other Stories

On the Cusp of Chaos

Dedicated to my mentor

Raymond T. Bell

world class entrepreneur and dear friend

The Art of Becoming An Entrepreneur

Table of Contents

Part One – The Idea

Launching a Trial Balloon

August 11th, 5 a.m.

It's the phone.

Four hours ago I was in Houston. Now I'm in bed - in Dallas! "Let it ring," I think.

"Come on," said a seemingly faraway voice after first answering the phone and having the briefest of conversations, "Get up!"

It was my wife. I wanted to say to her, "You can't do this to me! Today is my birthday. My body simply will not function before noon today."

"Come on, let's go," she insisted. "We're going for a hot air balloon ride!"

Well, that got me up all right, and it was off to the balloonport we sped. I was not only rousted out of bed before I was ready, I was even pressed into service to help prepare the hot air balloon for its launch! Before I knew it - before I really could catch my breath - we were several hundred feet above the forest on the north side of Dallas, Texas. With the sun just up, it was truly glorious. "I'M FLYING!" What an exhilarating feeling!

"Hold it! Why do I feel so wonderful?" Only 4 hours of sleep . . . Today's my birthday - and I deserve to sleep late .

. . And, I am afraid of flying.

There I was, up in a hot air balloon. I was tuckered out, a whole year older, and still scared to death of flying, at least in airplanes. Why was it, then, that I felt more alive at that moment than I had felt in many months?

When you can answer that question, you will understand how to successfully become an entrepreneur. You will also fully understand how to become successful at anything else in life that you are passionate about.

The Idea And What To Do With It

How many times have you had an idea for a new product, a new service, or a new business? How many times have you let those ideas slip from your mind with nothing having been done about them? Are these some of the reasons for your lack of action:

>   -The money needed was not there
>   -You didn't have the necessary skills
>   -Your friends talked you out of it
>   -All of your time was used up on other
>   things
>   -There were too many risks
>   -You didn't believe you could pull it off
>   -You just never seemed to get around to it

Do you recognize that list? Yes. It could go on and on, couldn't it?

Take the time necessary to read this book. Follow the step by step instructions. And never again will you have to think up excuses like those, above.

Now, let me tell you how this book came about.

Believe it or not, thinking about the art of hot air ballooning helped me to crystallize my thinking about the methods and the art of becoming an entrepreneur. Hot air ballooning is not for everyone, just as being an entrepreneur is not for everyone. In piloting a hot air balloon, your very life depends upon your piloting skills, and upon your ability to concentrate on the application of those skills to the job of keeping your balloon in flight. It takes concentration, dedication, and skill to fly a hot air balloon. It takes concentration, dedication, and skill to fly a business. The struggle to keep aloft is tough. The flight is long. The cause is noble.

My thoughts about flying in a hot air balloon were really exciting to me. Your ideas as to your entrepreneurial business must equally excite you, for if you become truly excited, you are almost bound to win.

What about skills verses fears? I have a terrible fear of flying in commercial aircraft. This has been explained to me as being due to the fact that I probably prefer to be in control of my own surroundings - to not be at the mercy of other people about whose skills I know little or nothing. I don't know if that explanation is really the correct one, but I do know that I don't like riding in airplanes. What, then, induced me to climb into the wicker basket of a hot air balloon and let myself be dragged skyward?

Probably, one of the reasons was that for more than a year before my first flight, I had been thinking that a ride in a hot air balloon, floating lazily over the countryside, would be exactly the kind of experience I was craving. I felt that it would be peaceful, refreshing, romantic, and something completely out of the ordinary. The "out of the ordinary" part excited me. The other thoughts soothed my flying fears. Thus, I kept seeing myself in that wicker basket, hand upraised to turn on the burner control, eyes alternating between the altimeter and the peacefully moving scene below. I let my dreams excite me even more as the months went on.

If you are serious about becoming an entrepreneur, the ideas from which your business will begin must be every bit as exciting to you as my ballooning ideas were to me. They cannot simply be whims or passing fancies. There must be a virtual obsession about the whole thing such that your ideas come to dominate your waking thoughts and your subconscious mind as well. The original ideas must build to the point where they will carry you through the rough air and storms that lie ahead.

How can you develop those original ideas and thoughts into that which becomes the driving force of your life? Probably there are many good ways by which you can do this, but the ways that I have found to be most useful during the early stages of a new venture are listed on the following pages.

Step One: Become Aware Of Your Choices

"Few people think more than two or three times a year. I have made an international reputation for myself by thinking once or twice a week."
George Bernard Shaw

Did you know that the average individual is said to have over 1,000 new ideas every day? Psychologists have discovered that most of us have more than 10,000 thoughts or ideas every week. With so many new ideas each day, it is no wonder that we get to act on so few of them. After all, if there are thousands of new ideas to sort through, how can we find the time to test all of them so as to pick out that one great, new idea that is just itching to be developed?

Begin by reading as much as you can about those things that interest you the most. If skiing is your interest, read ski books and ski magazines. If it is sailing, read sailing stories. If your interest is in computers, read everything you can find about computers. For an interest in people, read biographies. The more you read within your interest area, the better chance there will be for your main ideas to begin crystallizing.

Here are some reasons for concentrating your reading only in those areas in which you are most interested. To begin with, reading will boost your excitement about your new venture to the multi-hundred percent level. This high level of excitement will help you to follow through to the completion of your project. Another reason is that you can enter into a particular field and test it out through your reading. For example, you shouldn't work and save for twenty or thirty long years to be able to afford that sailboat of your dreams. Your reading should be able to help you find a better and faster way to get involved in sail boating. You shouldn't slave away until you can afford to pay for a ski trip. Read. Find some way to get into the skiing business.

Some people go into a bookstore and head straight for a book that was recommended by a friend, or perhaps a book on the bestseller list that week. They pass by novels, cookbooks, books on crafts, adventure, medicine, and so on - books in which they really have an interest. Why not forget about the bestsellers? Go for the book that will spark your imagination. Never underestimate the power of a book. They help you become aware of all of your many choices. Reading will help you explore and become excited. It is easy to do. Take the time to do it.

Once I was at breakfast in a hotel dining room. At the next table sat an elderly couple, travelers from their appearance. They asked the waitress for directions to the next city, a city of some size and but fifty miles away. It astounded me when the waitress told the couple that she had no idea of how they might get to that nearby city. "I have some friends who went there, but I don't know how they went!" The thought struck me that here was a girl who would be a waitress all of her life. It is one thing to not be able to afford to go places. It is quite another thing to not know how to get to them, afford the trip or not, and it is yet another thing to not fully understand that other places exist. This was a girl without a dream, without an idea, without reading.

Are you prepared to serve the same table for the rest of your life simply because you lack a road map? Every public library has maps. They won't come to you. You have to go to them. Why don't you begin planning YOUR trip today? As Mark Twain once said, "The man who does not read has no advantage over the man who cannot read."

To venture out on your own, you must first have an idea of the direction in which you will travel and of the options you will find along the way. But lack of information can do more to stop you in your tracks than will lack of money. For example, I have a friend who does not have a formal education. She has trouble reading and writing. Yet, she is one of the more skilled salespersons I have ever encountered. She got off to a fantastic start in her selling career, only to quit after a short time. "I just didn't feel that it was right for me."

The truth is, however, that she loved the selling, but she felt inferior to the other salespeople when it came to filling out the monthly sales reports. She lacked knowledge of what most of us consider to be the (to us) simple skills of reading and writing. Lack of knowledge leads directly to lack of self-confidence. Without self-confidence, people will come up against a lot of dead ends.

Now don't get so carried away with acquiring knowledge that you never get started doing what your ideas lead you to do. Begin gathering enough information to expand your thinking to the point where your earlier opinions no longer hold you back. Read more. Continue to learn. Just as your body needs physical exercise to stay fit, your mind needs mental exercise to become even fitter. Reading provides for your mind that which physical exercise provides for your body,

Most of America's greatest business and political leaders acquired the habit of reading everything they could about their various fields of interest. They read throughout their lives. So, if you want to be a success, begin by learning more about the things that interest you most. READ! You will be amazed at how this simple step will help you put new ideas into your mind, and how it will then help you sort them all out.

Step Two: Dream Big! Think Big!

"Restlessness and discontent are the first necessities of progress."
Thomas A. Edison

Think about how most of the successful people you know always seem to be excited about life's possibilities. Aren't these the people who can't wait to get up out of bed to meet the challenges of the coming day? You never hear these people say, "It's been Monday all day long!" or "Thank God it's Friday." Think about that. Have you ever heard a really successful person make a statement like either of those? No. Those are the kinds of things you hear from people who simply grind out a day-to-day living from their jobs. People who are genuinely happy with life don't talk like that because they don't think like that.

Why is it that so many people do say negative things about their daily lives? I believe that the majority of people still lead lives of desperation - not quiet desperation - for the complaints are loud. This is truly a tragedy. There is no need to live that way. Most people are probably unhappy because they have yet to find the right occupation. People who don't know what it is that they want to do with their lives are, without much doubt, among the least happy of all unhappy people.

This does not mean that you must have a plan for your life that covers every day for the next twenty years. That would be a mistake. For example, my high school counselor told me that I was destined to become a total failure if I did not

17

know exactly what I wanted to do with my life by the time I reached the age of sixteen. I guess that I am now in deep trouble. I really like the idea of changing professions every five or six years. Five or six years goes by all too fast when you are enjoying each day as much as I do.

The school counselor was wrong. I believe that the secret of a happy and successful life is to be able to spend your days doing work that gives you real satisfaction. If you lose your enthusiasm for one type of work you should move on to other things. If you work for someone else, don't marry your job. If you marry your job, it will take a messy divorce for you to be able to leave it. Instead, if you come to dislike your job you should be able to simply up and quit it. For those who work for others, that is good advice. For the entrepreneur, however, there is a marriage between the person and the work. There is the same type of commitment to the new enterprise as one makes to a spouse. The business must be exciting to almost the same degree as a spouse is exciting. If not, the attempt to be an entrepreneur will be a bitter experience instead of a joy.

As you develop your big idea, try to be as creative and as innovative as possible. It is all right to follow the successful ideas of other people, but you should do as much as you can to make the idea unique again so that it becomes truly yours. Amazingly, people seem to copy bad ideas more than they copy good, successful ideas. A restaurant will go out of business only to be followed by another restaurant in the same location that also goes out of business. Beaten paths are for beaten people. So, start off with a good idea and expand on it. Don't just copy. Creatively copy. Use not only your objective intellect, but also your instinct and intuition. Think things through with as much reason and logic as possible, but don't reject an idea just because it doesn't fit into some popular concept of how things should be done. Everyone has these instinctive powers in addition to ordinary reasoning powers. They are gifts. Use them.

It has been said that five percent of the people do the real thinking - ten percent think they think - and the remainder would rather die than think. If that saying is true, then it is the five percent who change things. While you may not consider your mind to be a great one, your ideas are quite capable of producing massive effects - on individuals, on society, and on things in general. Do you remember the hula hoop? No one would claim that it required a person with an advanced academic degree to come up with the hula hoop. After all, a hoop is just a hoop - and hoops have been around for kids to play with for centuries. The idea to promote "Hula Hooping" was a catchy idea. It worked. So can your ideas. Everyone has had at least one idea that beats the little idea behind the hula hoop. So - when are we going to hear about your ideas?

What is it for which you want to become known? Take a stand at the start of your new enterprise - hold onto or bring back the dreams of your youth. Nothing is going to stop you this time. You are doing this for YOU. If you make yourself happy, you can make the world a better place for all of us.

Today is the beginning! What stand will you take today? You are going to place yourself in that five percent of the people who actually take the time to think about where they are going and what it is that they really desire to accomplish. It is not always easy to stop long enough to actually think, nor will anyone pay you to simply think, but if you do not spend at least a little time every day in peaceful thought you will rob yourself and your new enterprise of that most valuable asset - ideas. So, after you dream, then you must think. After you think, then you must act.

For some people, the best ideas occur when showering. For others, the ideas come along during driving, sleeping, or exercising. The time for a good idea to come to a person is when that person is not otherwise involved with business or with problems. Showering, jogging, driving, and the like are not quiet times, but they are mental quiet times - the times when the best ideas usually come to those who think. Good ideas don't always surface during long, high-pressure meetings. The big ideas, the really good ones, often surface when you let them rise to the top without a lot of pressure and strain.

How many times have you had an idea that, early on, seemed to hold great promise, yet you did nothing about it? If you are like most of us, this sort of thing happens frequently. All too often you meet up with your idea again - but somewhere else.

"You know, I thought of that a year ago, but I didn't follow up on it because..."

Well, why didn't you follow up on that good idea?

"There was no way in which I could control the situation - I had no money - I had no time - I couldn't figure out what to do next."

The Art of Becoming An Entrepreneur

Of all miseries, the bitterest is to feel so much and to have control over so little. Actually you have much more control than you might believe. You, and only you, are in control of your own thoughts. You have complete authority over your thoughts. It is your one area of complete control - complete freedom. Rarely will a day go by without a winning idea popping into someone's head. However, as Mark Twain said, "Fortune knocks at every man's door at least once in a lifetime, but in a good many cases the man is in a neighboring saloon and does not hear her."

Be at home when Fortune knocks!

Most wage earners do not like to vary procedures. You might even come to believe that some people, if not most of them, stopped thinking the minute they signed on to work for someone else. Murray Spangler, however, was a wage earner who was different. Murray began his career as a janitor in a department store in the city of Canton, Ohio. Murray had the idea that dust could be kept down whenever the floors were being swept. That was Murray's idea. Later, he came up with a plan. He convinced a friend to finance his plan. No doubt, you have heard of Murray's friend - A. W. Hoover - the Hoover vacuum cleaner man. Murray wanted to vary procedures. Murray didn't like dust. If you are a wage earner and want to become an entrepreneur, learn to hate dust!

Once I worked for someone I called the "man with the Midas touch." He worked at a chemical plant. One day, a pipe carrying molten sulfur became clogged - frozen. Remelting sulfur required a lot of heat, but even wrapping the sulfur-filled pipe with steam tubes didn't do the job. My former boss came up with the idea of mixing graphite with cement and packing the mixture around the steam tubes. The idea worked. The sulfur remelted. The "Man with the Midas Touch" started a new business based on this idea and his company, Thermon Manufacturing Company, is now known the world over. He didn't let his big idea pass him by.

If you are going to become a successful entrepreneur, your idea must be big enough to totally capture your mind. It must be a BIG dream. Ideas belong to everyone - and so your big idea does not necessarily have to have originated with you! Remember all of those ideas you had (and let pass on by) that were acted upon by someone else? Your goal should be to act upon your most exciting idea. If the project excites you - if it is FUN - then you will need no excuses. You already have everything you need to get started, as you will soon discover.

There are times when a person must do those things that one has to do. Now, however, it is time for you to start doing those things that you LIKE to do. What is it that you enjoy doing more than anything else? Be slow to answer. Mistrust the obvious.

The real tragedy of life is not death - the ending - it is that so may people die inside while yet alive. Don't become one of the living dead. Think! Dream! Use your imagination to the fullest. Lock onto a new dream, and make it a daring one.

Dream big. Think big. And you will live a magnificent life.

Step Three: Don't Reject An Idea That At First Seems Impossible

"In every work of genius we recognize our own rejected thoughts; they come back to us with a certain alienated majesty."
Ralph Waldo Emerson

How many of your good ideas have you discarded only to later see them implemented by others? When I was in the Navy, a friend and I had what we called brainstorming sessions. Each week we would come up with a new "million dollar idea." Sadly, we never implemented any of those ideas. Instead, we both took normal paths after leaving the service. Since then, however, several of our "million dollar ideas" have been put into use by others, earning for the people who implemented them significant amounts of money. Seeing others succeed with, "my" ideas was one of the reasons for my eventually breaking away and beginning my own business.

In the form in which most good ideas originate, they quite often seem to be impossible - and so they are immediately rejected. Entrepreneurs, on the other hand, are those who follow through with these impossible ideas. These are the people who change the world. An original idea is a lot like an eagle's egg. Entrepreneurs look at the outside of the egg and envision a great bird soaring high in the sky. The entrepreneur understands well the dangers and difficulties that must be overcome before that bird can soar, but the successful flight of that bird can be clearly seen.

There have probably been more good ideas lost due to misplaced fears about what might go wrong along the way than due to any other cause. Your idea may not be perfect, and something could go wrong, but those are not good reasons for rejecting an idea. The business people with the best reputations are those who search for things to do that "cannot be done" - and who then do them.

It is a fact that nothing useful would ever be accomplished if all possible objections had to be overcome first. When they first emerge, most good ideas tend to be of the impossible variety. Some people call these ideas "dreams." So go ahead with the Big Dream! Don't reject it because it has some flaws or because something could go wrong. Think it through. Put everyone on notice that you prefer to fail at something great rather than to succeed at something small.

Step Four: Don't Wait For Everything To Be Perfect Before You Begin

"Nothing will ever be attempted if all possible objections must be first overcome."
Samuel Johnson

Entertainer Oscar Levant once said, "Once I make up my mind, I'm full of indecision."

He might have been talking for the rest of us. Today, when there seem to be more opportunities, more choices, available than ever before, so many of us seem to be paralyzed with indecision. Those good ideas that you had last year and the year before are perhaps still nothing more than good ideas. Why haven't you put them into action?

Many people fear failure of performance (not just losing money) so much that they delay beginning a new venture until they have planned every minute detail. While there is nothing wrong with detailed planning, it is important to DO SOMETHING with an exciting idea rather than to work on it until it becomes perfect. If you take the first step in getting organized (see Part Three) a beneficial chain of events will be started. Each of your early thoughts will begin to grow as your initial organization develops. Each of your thoughts might breed ten new thoughts, and those in turn may go on to show you whole new vistas not even dreamed of when you started.

People tend to spend so much time planning in their attempts to eliminate all chances of failure that they also

25

fail to recognize new, unconventional approaches, the kinds of approaches that seem to appear most often when the entrepreneur is actually "under fire." Yes, there are times when meticulous planning is absolutely essential. The planning for a space shuttle launch is a good example. Most new ventures, however, are not of the magnitude of the space program. So do only the planning absolutely necessary (as described in Part Three) and then get started and let your creative energy take over as the scenario develops.

Charles Goodyear worked for years to develop waterproof garments using rubber. Goodyear didn't attempt to think the entire process through before the first experiment. He had his idea. He started his project. While showing some friends unsuccessful results of his tests, Goodyear created quite a stink by accidentally dropping a piece of rubber onto a hot surface. Can't you hear his friends right now? "Goodyear, why don't you quit playing around and get yourself a normal job?"

Well, Goodyear tossed that stinky piece of heated rubber outdoors so that his laboratory would not smell so bad. He retrieved that piece of rubber the next morning so that he might properly discard it into the trash barrel. To his surprise, the rubber had not lost its pliability, and it was firmly attached to the pot lid onto which it had dropped the night before. Nowadays, we call that process vulcanizing. Was Goodyear's discovery actually an accident? No. He was actively engaged in his little research business. The "accident" occurred because of his actions. Had Goodyear still been planning on what to do, the chances are slim to none that he could have discovered the process of vulcanization. There are many other examples similar to this. People like Goodyear seem to have one thing in common - their ideas arrived, were considered rapidly, and were acted upon before all the minute details could be worked out.

Only in the arena of action can you sort out the really essential parts of your plan. That is why it is important to get into action just as soon as you have taken care of the basics. It might surprise you to learn of how much information you already possess, and of how much preparation you have already completed.

Who knows what great discovery you might make if only you will begin. Do you remember the story of how America was "discovered" by the Europeans? When it was finally discovered, it was unwanted! For the next fifty years additional exploration was performed in the hope of getting through or around it. And keep in mind that America was not discovered and populated by people who stayed behind in Europe. What might you discover once you get started?

Throughout history a vast portion of truth and new discovery has come from the seemingly irrelevant. Those who think too much before acting will likely decide their ideas are not workable. The rewards, however, go to those people who DO things with their ideas. Don't spend unnecessary time analyzing your dreams - live them.

Step Five: Don't Worry About What Other People Are Thinking

"For an idea that does not at first seem insane, there is no

hope."
Albert Einstein

Your every new idea, at its inception, has but one supporter - you! Now you have to sell that idea to other people. It doesn't matter how good your idea may be - you, the originator, must go forward and convince others to adopt it. This is true for a new scientific discovery or for a new business plan. You will find that few people, if any, initially think your idea to be good. People tend to reject ideas they don't themselves conceive. Another thing - it is natural for others to see all the flaws and potential problems first, and then realize the beauty of your new idea only later. For those reasons, your new venture must be based on an idea so exciting to you that you can move forward despite the negativity you may encounter early on.

When you first begin presenting your new idea to friends, neighbors, and relatives, be prepared to receive only negative comments about your plans. If everyone immediately thinks you have a great idea you had better think it through again - something is wrong with it. A handy rule of thumb is that if your neighbors think that you and your idea are nuts, then you just may be on the right track. Obviously, there are many exceptions to this cynical viewpoint, but you should be prepared for a lot of rejection before your new idea begins to gain acceptance.

Also, in the beginning, you should be wary of the so-called experts, or consultants. Experts and consultants can often provide excellent guidance as your venture progresses, but it is risky to have them around your ideas while those ideas are still in the formative stages. If you want some instant negative criticism, just tell an expert what you have in mind to do. There will be an onslaught of criticism, but if you are prepared for it you can come out of the encounter stronger and with an idea that may have received some fine tuning that you might not have been able to provide without the criticism. Even though exposing your new idea can be a painful experience, it is well worth the pain. Most ideas seem to grow better when transplanted into other minds.

Don't worry about the fact that not everyone is going to accept your new idea. That doesn't necessarily mean that it is a bad idea. It just means that you have hit on something that isn't common. That isn't bad. It is good. There is great beauty in every idea, but not everyone is able to see the beauty. Try to not waste too much time trying to convince everyone that your idea is a great idea. The only people who really need to be convinced are the ones without whom your idea will not work. In most ventures there are only a few people really central to its success. These people must be sold on your idea. Leave the convincing of the rest of the world until later.

You have probably noticed that progress is never created by contented people. You will also find that there is no such thing as a contented entrepreneur. It is not that entrepreneurs do not become satisfied with their creations. It is that a true entrepreneur is continually searching for the new, the different, the exciting idea.

Remember, all great ideas begin within a single mind. It takes a lot of effort on your part to simply get your idea accepted by a limited number of selected people. Don't be concerned by those who first reject your idea. Instead, concern yourself with those who encourage you and provide you moral and financial help and support. Those are the people who understand what you are going through and how important it is to support new ideas. Later, after you have achieved success, you will be amazed by the fact that everyone who earlier rejected your ideas will try to take at least some credit for your success. Smile and say, "Thank you."

Around the year 1900 an obscure inventor built a new racing car. He called it "999." The inventor hired a little-known professional cyclist named Barney Oldfield to drive "999" in an automobile race. They won the race with previously unheard of speeds of 60 miles an hour. This win launched the careers of both men.

Years later, the auto builder encountered Oldfield and generously confessed, "There's no denying it, Barney, you made me and I made you."

"That's true," joked Oldfield, "but to be quite honest about it, Mr. Ford, you must admit that I did a much better job making you than you did making me."

You will encounter many Barney Oldfields in your life. Love them. They make life interesting.

Step Six: Don't Think You Can't Do It. You Can

"When God gives man an office, He gives him brains enough to fill it"
German proverb

The Art of Becoming An Entrepreneur

Too often I have heard people say, "If only I were smarter (or taller, or smaller, or thinner, or richer...) I could do that."

Whenever people start to say, "If only I ...," you know that someone is throwing in the towel due to the lack of a sufficiently positive self image.

Poor self image may be the most significant reason that many new ideas never get off the ground. Right here and now you must realize that you can do it. You can do whatever it takes to get that idea moving. You are an entrepreneur. Nothing can stop you. By putting aside all doubts about your abilities you can begin to grow into whatever image you want to have of yourself. Get rid of any negative notions about your own abilities and you will be surprised at the results.

Did you know that by using less than half your brain you can:

> -Memorize a major encyclopedia from A to Z
> -Learn over 40 different languages
> -Sense (feel) projections 1/25,000 of an inch on apparently smooth surfaces
> -Detect one part quinine in 2 million parts of water
> -Identify over 10,000 odors

And all of those functions use less than half of your brain! Amazing! What are you waiting for? You have few limits other than those you place on yourself.

One of the reasons so many good ideas are lost is that the

people who have the ideas lack the self-confidence required to follow through with them. Although self-confidence will be discussed in a later chapter, it may be appropriate to consider now the reasons why lack of self-confidence is a major idea killer.

Most people experience an almost godlike sensation of being able to conquer the world as they pass through their late teens and into their early twenties. It is during that period of a person's life that there is a strong belief that he or she can do anything if the desire is there. It is during that period when many people forge their life plans and begin to follow those plans. However, it is also during that period that most people have to enter the "cold, cruel world." That entrance causes far too many people to lose the dreams of their youth. How much more wonderful this world would be if everyone could retain their youthful dreams, and follow through on an upbeat life plan. What happens to people to prevent this?

For some people it is getting married and having to face the harsh economic realities of life. For others, there may be a sense of being left behind - of starting too late. I went through a period like this myself just as I graduated from college. Through luck I secured a job as a stuntman in the movie "Hawaii." Julie Andrews starred in that movie. During its filming I met Miss Andrews and discovered what a charming person she is. She is very much like you and me. This was, at first, an exciting discovery, but it soon depressed me. You see, at that time Miss Andrews was twenty-seven years old, just five years older than me at the time. She was already known the world over, and there I was, a young nobody. All of the accomplishments of which

I had been so proud vanished into thin air as I realized that I hadn't accomplished a fraction of what she had done by my age.

This discontent - this unhappiness - lasted several years. Now I can look back at all I had accomplished during those days and again be happy and proud. Maybe I wasn't world famous, but in my own way I had done as much in my life up to that point as had Julie Andrews in hers. The real difference was that I knew what she had done, and very few people knew what I had done. The key to overcoming my depression was to feel good about all of the things I HAD DONE, and to not dwell on what I had yet to accomplish. It didn't matter how many other people knew of my accomplishments as long as I was satisfied with them and with myself. It no longer mattered to me if anyone else ever knew.

The important thing in life is that your dream be big enough and exciting enough to completely capture your *own* imagination and cause *you* to feel good about what you are doing.

Do you remember the main premise of this section? Make your idea so big that you forget about everything else. The enthusiasm generated by such an idea is like a high voltage current that keeps your motor running at top speed. If you look close enough, you will find that at the core of every great business there is a single individual who is still consumed with enthusiasm for his or her project.

Such enthusiasm will not only keep your idea alive, it will also help to keep you alive. You will find, no matter your age at the time you started your business, that your aging will seem to cease just as long as the excitement and enthusiasm remain - indeed, you will feel young again. Age is not really measured in years. It is measured by temperament. I am acquainted with twenty year olds who are old, and I know octogenarians who are young. Get excited. Take a chance. Grab the opportunity. Go for it!

A person's greatest enemies are his or her own apathy and closed mindedness. As an entrepreneur you must free your mind of the shackles of past defeats and shortcomings. Don't pine for opportunities lost. Look instead to the opportunities you are creating - for yourself and for others. There are a great many people who might benefit from opportunities that do not yet exist - but that you will create. It is up to you to see to it that they come into existence. Do not worry about your talents or lack of them. You are what you are.

You will find that the primary requirement of being an entrepreneur is not talent, but willpower. Start working on your willpower by nourishing your new idea. Let it grow. Let it develop in your mind. Let it excite you. That is the beginning - the beginning of a new business, a new product, a new work of art, a new book. Whatever may be the idea, it is the beginning of something that the Earth has not seen before. This is your idea and it is your responsibility to bring it forth into the world. You are its creator. Don't let your dream die. Reject bad ideas, but latch onto your great ideas and bring them forth. Don't allow any present lack of self-confidence to stop you. Don't stop before you begin. It is criminal to allow yourself to be humbled into poverty and obscurity. You are better than that. You have all the talent you need to become an entrepreneur. You have your mind and your dreams. All of the other talents you can learn or you can hire.

Step Seven: Don't Reject Ideas Because Things Could Go Wrong

"The concessions of the weak are the concessions of fear."
Edmund Burke

How often have you started working on a good idea and then, after a day or two, cast it away because all you could see were the problems? More ideas are rejected because of potential problems than are rejected for other reasons. Ours has become a nation dedicated to the elimination of problems, and therefore most people don't think an idea has merit if it also has a number of problems associated with it. This is indeed unfortunate. Obviously we are never going to eliminate all problems in this life. Yet we so often destroy the foundations of future solutions because we don't want to cope with problems.

Have you ever noticed how many more success stories there are about first and second generation Americans than there are about people whose families have lived in America for several generations? I believe the reason for this is that a family just arriving on our shores sees nothing but unlimited opportunity. By the third or fourth generation the family begins to shift from a posture of grasping opportunities to "holding onto what we have." The striving becomes one of reaching for security rather than reaching for opportunity.

It is both the calling and the duty of the entrepreneur to look beyond the problems and to visualize the hoped for results of their dreams. One reason an entrepreneur needs to have big, exciting ideas is that without ideas being on a grand scale, problems may soon overpower the ideas. To be successful you must do as our forefathers did when they first arrived in this golden land. You must dream new dreams. Set the world on notice that you are ready to fail at something great rather than succeed at something small. Greatness is built by searching for tasks that seem impossible and then doing them. How great are you going to become?

If your idea were without problems many other people would have already begun working on it. Psychological tests now show that similar thought patterns circle the globe at lightning speed and allow a number of people to receive them at the same time. One example of this can be seen when a Nobel prize is shared by two people working in the same field at the same time - and for work that is almost identical. They need not have studied each others' work. When an idea begins to form in one mind it becomes accessible to others, and soon it is available to all minds in the world. So don't wait to work out all the little problems that you see before you. If you wait too long your idea will come back to haunt you in the form of someone else's work.

Doctor Robert Schuler gave advice on this subject: "When God gives you a dream it will seem impossible. That is the only kind of dream there is. But one should never reject a potentially great idea, and never reject an idea because it's not your way of doing things."

That is excellent advice - difficult to follow, but excellent. If you think that you must first overcome all possible objections, you will never attempt anything. This is why it is so important that you be careful in selecting people with whom to work - your key people. As an organization develops it can survive one or two negative thinkers who might be on the scene, but it can be fatal in the early years if some of your key people have negative strains. The way to spot these people is by their first reactions and responses to whatever it is that you propose.

A man once worked for me who would respond with "It can't be done!" to everything I might suggest. Invariably, he would return to me a few hours later and tell me that he had been correct earlier - it couldn't be done - but nonetheless he had found a way to do it. Until I realized that this person always reacted the same way, seeing the impossibility of a situation rather than its sometimes hidden possibilities, I avoided telling him about our future plans because his constant negativity was becoming demoralizing to me.

At that same time there was a person on our staff who instantly got excited about any idea that was proposed and immediately went to work on it. Very often she would return with news of a potential problem, some of which were so great that the idea had to be scrapped. Yet she was a very important member of our staff because she explored the potential of new ideas without first focusing on the problems they might cause. People who concentrate on problems first are often doomed to failure, or at the very least, they lower the moral of an enterprise to sometimes dangerous levels.

Step Eight: Forget About Money! Work On The Idea

"Do what you can with what you have where you are."
Theodore Roosevelt

It has been my experience that once a person has an idea that is really exciting, money begins to follow that idea. The idea may not be exciting to the first twenty or thirty people to whom it is presented, but if the idea is exciting to its originator it will eventually attract the money needed to bring it to full life. Martin Luther said that everything done in the world is done by hope. Nothing could be truer as to how the ideas of an entrepreneur take root and grow. If you are serious about becoming an entrepreneur you will find the means to bring your ideas to life. If the means are not readily to be found, you will somehow create the means.

In a later section of this book we will deal more thoroughly with the subject of raising and using capital, but it is important that you realize right from the beginning that money is not going to be your problem. Often I have seen an aspiring entrepreneur spend weeks trying to figure out how little he or she could give for every dollar of capital raised. People like this often end up with nothing. If the effort had been, instead, to figure out how MUCH could be given for every dollar raised, there would have been no money problems. I don't mean that one has to give away all, or a large part of a new venture. What I mean is that one must be completely fair to everyone concerned: customers, suppliers, stockholders, and yourself and your family.

In addition to the realization that you don't have problems with money, it is important to understand two other truths while you are still in the formulative stages of your new idea:

> -The end does not justify the means.
> -The engine that will keep your venture going is profit.

There are many examples in the business world of entrepreneurs wanting seed capital so badly that they sell their souls to the devil. Remember, once you accept money from someone, you are bound to them until they leave the venture. Be sure that they are the kind of people with whom you enjoy working.

It is also important to understand from the beginning that you must eventually make a profit if you are to succeed. No matter how thrifty you are or how much you keep the overhead down in the beginning, somewhere down the line your business must become profitable. A great idea that doesn't generate a profit is simply not a great business idea.

And keep in mind that pursuing a profit doesn't mean that you must become a greedy capitalist. It is what you do with the profits of your venture that determines the kind of person you actually are. If you share your profits equitably with your employees, your customers, the community in which your business is situated, and lastly, with your shareholders, then you will surely be known as a good-hearted person, a philanthropist, perhaps. Only if you keep all of the profits to yourself will you begin to slip into the pit of greed and avarice.

Should your new enterprise ever grow to where it needs an infusion of capital through the issuing of shares of ownership to the general public, I highly recommend that you read Marjorie Kelly's brilliant book, _The Divine Right of Capital: Dethroning the Corporate Aristocracy_, and put into practice some of her excellent suggestions, particularly those about a corporation's responsibility to its employees, customers, and community relative to the rights of its distant shareholders. As you will see from Kelly's work, corporations do not of necessity have to be anti-human institutions.

Step Nine: Take A Chance

"Fear not that thy life shall come to an end, but rather fear that it shall never have a beginning."
Cardinal Newman

Periodically we see a news story about someone who attempts suicide by jumping off of a high building. Friends try to talk the person out of jumping. Below, we feel the tension and the anguish of the person on the ledge as he or she thinks over the situation. If you have ever wondered what goes on in the mind of that person on the ledge, you can now stop wondering. YOU are that person.

The person on the ledge has but two choices - jump or don't jump. Either decision is irrevocable. Entrepreneurs have the same two choices - also irrevocable. But, no matter the decision you make, it is much better than sitting on a ledge suffering the leap over and over again. By the time you finish reading this book you will have finished your ledge-sitting career. It will then be time for you to take charge of your own life. Go ahead. Jump. Take a chance.

People are often robbed by two thieves - regret of yesterday and fear of tomorrow. Have you been consistently rejecting good ideas simply because there is risk involved? If so then you had better take a close look at what it is that you fear to lose. The fear of taking a chance implies that you have something to lose. Do you really have something to lose? Of course you do - everyone does, but I will give you a list of some things that really deserve your fear:

> The government
> Political parties
> Junior chambers of commerce
> Payroll deductions
> Insurance programs
> Credit cards
> Retirement benefits
> Time clocks
> Time payments
> Television
> Newspapers, and
> Prepaid cemetery plots

Now there is a list of things to fear. So spend your time being afraid of the things on that list, and then you won't have time left to fear whatever else might cause you to reject new ideas.

You must have more faith in yourself. It doesn't really matter all that much should you lose everything you now own. You acquired it once before, and you can acquire it all once again. It is essential to your well being that you ignore risks and begin to take your solo flight. Every person worth his or her salt has an inborn desire to solo. Do you want to fly, to sing, to write, to cook, to dance, to explore, to paint, to invent? When you find the one area where you most want to fly solo, then go for it. Forget the risk and fly. Surely you must be getting tired of sitting on that ledge by now.

So here you are at a major turning point in your life. Simply by reading this book you have shown to yourself that the spark is there. You know that an entrepreneur is somewhere inside you, struggling to get out. The time has now arrived to bring that entrepreneur out into the daylight so as to see what can be made of him or her. It is time to quit carrying around someone else's bags and to pick up your own. Like it or not, no one will ever care what you "could have done." All that really matters is what you actually do. You are ready to go on the greatest voyage of your life. Don't miss the boat.

Step Ten: Begin Today

"Thinking without constructive action becomes a disease."
Henry Ford

I have a friend who constantly comes up with new stories that tell of the great things he has done in the past. To hear him talk, my friend could run any business in the country - yet he makes his living by doing odd jobs. The man is extremely likable, and is even believable, yet I have never actually seen him accomplish anything. What he doesn't understand is that the world doesn't need people to tell big stories. What the world needs is people who will do big deeds.

Your having spent a number of years gaining some special knowledge will not, in itself, do you all that much good. It is only the application of your knowledge that will bring you success. You can't build your reputation on what you are going to do, but only on what you are doing or have already done. So stop thinking about it and DO it. You aren't lacking in capacity. Few people are. What most people lack is application. If you don't do something about your ideas today, those ideas may never become any larger than the brain cells they now occupy. Act! Having a good idea is not nearly as important as acting on one once it comes to you.

How many times have you seen a sign that says, "Do It Now"? Those three words are, without a doubt, among the more important words an entrepreneur may read, hear, or say. DO IT NOW! Most people cannot overcome a constant inclination to do nothing. It is certainly easier to let things happen than it is to make things happen, yet the concept central to being an entrepreneur is that of making things happen. So you see, that makes it all much easier for you - there is so little competition.

While your friends, neighbors, relatives, and co-workers talk about the great accomplishments of others, why don't you forget about all of the talking and go ahead and accomplish something instead. Start today. Rarely has caution ever created a great fortune. Action is the ingredient required to begin a new venture. It isn't knowledge. It isn't money. It isn't the right connections. It is action that is required - almost before all else. You don't need to be a genius to become an entrepreneur. There already is sufficient genius in your energy and activity. If you are to succeed, you will need a sense of urgency about getting things done. So start right now. Don't wait until you have finished reading this book. Begin your new enterprise by taking the following steps - NOW:

1. Write down the central idea of your proposed new business.

2. Write down exactly what it is you wish to get out of your business if everything goes according to plan.

3. Write down what you think it will take in terms of time, energy, and family sacrifice to get through the first two years.

4. Write down a list of people whom you think will be needed to help you.

Stop right now and take those four steps. It is essential that you take those steps now, not later today, not tomorrow but NOW. It is also essential that you do not yet begin to share your ideas with anyone, not even with the people whose help you will need. Your ideas must be fortified before you begin to expose them in public, but when you take the four steps listed above, you are on your way. You have decided that, this time, it is your turn to go for it.

Summary of Part One: The Idea

1. Become aware of your choices

2. Think. Think about BIG dreams

3. Don't reject ideas that at first seem impossible

4. Don't wait for everything to be perfect before beginning

5. Don't worry about what other people are thinking

6. Don't think you can't do it. You can

7. Don't reject an idea because something could go wrong

8. Forget about money; work on the idea

9. Take a chance

10. Begin TODAY

Part Two – Refining The Idea

Will the Bubble Burst?

August 20th.

On six of the past ten mornings I have crewed for the pilot who took me for my first balloon ride. My decision to buy a balloon has been made and has caused some problems, mostly financial. I knew that I could get a loan, but there is little room in our budget for balloon payments. For certain, a balloon will cause me problems at home since there are things other than balloons that we need.

When I checked on the training required to obtain a license to pilot a balloon, I believed that I could qualify by the first day of October. I could then take my wife for a balloon ride on our anniversary. Some of the stories the pilots told scared me a little, but mainly I remembered the thrill of my first flight. Although I believe that I have made a final decision to buy a hot air balloon, I still have to think everything through for a few more days so that I might see if this balloon thing is more than just a passing fancy.

Step One: Expanding Your Idea

"*Our plans miscarry because they have no aim. When a man does not know what harbor he is making for, no wind*

is the right wind."
Seneca

Even though my excitement level in ballooning was extremely high, I knew that I had to work out all of the different problems that would arise if I went ahead with ballooning. At first, getting out of bed long before sunrise, plus the expense involved, seemed to be barriers to my carrying through with buying a balloon. But I continually came back to that first flight. It had been magnificent. Thus, I began to work through the problems. That is now what you must do with your new idea.

If you followed the instructions in Part One you should now have a single sheet of paper with four items written on it:

1. The central idea of your new business

2. Exactly what you want to get out of this business

3. What it will cost you in time, energy, and family sacrifice

4. Who will be needed to help you

Now take those four items and refine them. Keep in mind that while your central idea is still very general, it must also be so big and so exciting that accomplishing it seems almost impossible. For example, as I work on this book, I am also working on a business plan that may be impossible to accomplish, but I know that the principles of the bigness and excitement of an idea are backed by an immutable law that will be explained later in this section. That is why I am forging ahead with my own "impossible dream." Are you ready to go forward with your "impossible dream"?

Let's begin. Take a look at your main idea and see if it can be developed into something more concrete. Your new idea should be more than just a thought about how to make more money. It must be so BIG that it is constantly on your mind. Since such ideas also provide almost endless choices of action, the trick is to narrow that broad, central idea into a single, clearly focused plan of action.

The following example of a big idea may help explain the steps involved in refining your own big idea. Here goes: *I would like to earn a comfortable living through a pleasurable involvement with sailboats and sailing.*

Now you must list all of the choices you can think of that are available to you, so that you might accomplish that which your idea encompasses:

> *Sell sailboats*
> *Repair sailboats*
> *Operate a charter sailboat*
> *Write about sailboats*
> *Rent sailboats to others*
> *Design sailboats*

It isn't important how detailed your list of options is at this time. What is important is that, by assembling this information about your idea, you discover the range of possibilities available to you. It is important to look into as many aspects of sailboats and sail boating as possible - you may even find areas in which you are already very well equipped to begin a new business.

Look at your list of options and visualize yourself actually doing whatever that option requires of a person in order to earn money. For example, running a charter sailboat - you must picture not only the good times when you sail with a fair wind, you must also consider the times when you will have charter guests who are difficult to please - or who are just plain difficult, seasick, or who tell you what a bad job you are doing. If those thoughts give you real pause, cross the charter boat option off of the list. Then look at the next option, and so on.

Sometimes your search to discover all available options will lead you in unexpected directions. Consider the option, "design sailboats." When you jotted it down, you really didn't think that designing sailboats held any real promise for you. However, you should be trying to find out everything you possibly can find out about each one of your listed options. How do people become sailboat designers? Well, it turns out that there is an excellent school that specializes in a home correspondence course in sailboat designing. In fact, many famous boat designers have graduated from that school. If you had a flair for mechanical drawing in high school, this may be the option for you. The point is, you should not eliminate any possibility until it is fully explored. Don't discount your own capabilities too soon.

In your search for the right facet of your big idea to bring into reality, keep in mind that every person who looks at a particular venture sees it in a different light. Only by constant searching and studying will the best path be revealed. Earlier, I mentioned the Charles Goodyear story - it took Goodyear some time to discover the answer to his problems with the rubberizing of fabric, but the answer was there all the time. James Watt discovered the principles of using steam to power an engine - and many consider him a genius because of his discoveries. Remember, though, that he was looking for an answer. The natural laws that govern the workings of a steam engine have always existed, yet it took a James Watt to bring those laws into the light. There are still thousands and thousands of discoveries waiting for entrepreneurs to find. Some of these discoveries will involve science and nature, while others will involve the way people interact with one another. Might there be a discovery you will make that will help people live together in greater harmony? The natural laws have always been right there, waiting to be discovered and used. So, too, is the answer to your need to be independent. That answer won't come looking for you. You have to go out and find it for yourself.

One mistake that people make once they have decided to begin their own businesses is to rush into those businesses without first establishing overall objectives. Unfortunately, the times in which we are now living are characterized by attempts to perfect the means while confusing the goals. Years ago, nuclear energy seemed to promise an answer to all the earth's energy needs. We built a large number of successful nuclear power stations that provided lots of power in about as perfect a manner as one might hope. Unfortunately, no one seemed to be willing to work out the long term goals. As a result, we have a big problem on our hands concerning what to do with the spent radioactive wastes of these power plants, not to mention the problems that can arise when that spent fuel is stored on top of an earthquake fault zone. Isn't it too bad that we didn't spend more time and energy way back in the beginning to develop long term goals regarding energy. Had we done so, the billions of dollars wasted on poorly designed nuclear power plants could have been profitably spent developing solar plants, wind power generators, and tidal energy sources.

Don't let the lack of an overall objective move you in a wrong direction. Before you set out on your own new venture, and before you involve more people in that venture with you, make sure that you have your directions straight.

You might become tempted to begin working out a business plan, to tell your friends about your dream, and to get going. Instead, start with the basics. The first thing to do is to question and examine your underlying reason for embarking on the new venture. An unhappy millionaire is a person with a million dollars and no established reason for doing whatever is being done. So, thoroughly sort out all of the options before working on your business plan. Sure, get into action, but remember that thinking is also needed to build a successful venture. Albert Schweitzer put it this way: "The greatest problem we have today is that men simply don't think."

Entrepreneurs are generally pretty good thinkers - yet they have difficulty in finding time in which to think. The more successful they become, the scarcer becomes the time in which to do some quiet thinking. Now, before your battles begin, you are lucky - you can actually take the time needed to think about the various options available to you. You might put it this way - after the dream comes reality. So let that initial dream run wild. While your dream is exercising itself, don't feel that you are losing precious time that could be better spent in practicing what you are dreaming. One day you will see that all those hours spent dreaming and sorting out the options were the most valuable hours spent in the development of your enterprise.

As you examine your options, remember what you have already learned in part one:

> No idea is impossible
> You need not wait for everything to be perfect
> Don't reject an option because it has a few flaws
> Don't worry about money (yet!)

At this stage it is important to totally put your trust in your idea and to completely ignore your present circumstances. Put your mind to work on your idea. Be different than the majority of men and women who rarely use their greatest asset - the power of thought.

People may not like to stop and think because they don't feel any immediate sense of accomplishment for their effort. Yet, many of those same people spend much of their time reminiscing about past accomplishments. Remembering past events is fun. Thinking, imagining, and planning the future are much more rewarding. When you set your mind to work at imagining, your mind is moving in a forward direction. That is the direction in which entrepreneurs must go - forward.

While quietly thinking things through, be sure to have some paper and a pencil close at hand. Don't feel that you must write down every single thought that pops into your head, but, from time to time, you will have a bright flash of an idea that could be revolutionary. I am convinced that all great ideas appear in this way, and should you not grab them when they flash through your brain, they may be lost to you forever. You may want to keep note-writing materials by your bed. I often have a dream that seems to have one kernel of reality to it. That little kernel could later be important. If I don't write it down as soon as I wake up it will be gone.

As you begin to sort through your options you will find a pleasant change taking place in your life. First of all, you will feel lighter and freer than you have felt in years. Secondly, the people closest to you will begin to be much happier for the simple reason that they are reflecting your happier mood. If you are concerned about making others happy then get happy with yourself first. Others will just naturally follow your lead.

One of the reasons this new lightness occurs is that you have begun to throw off the chains of boredom. Humankind was not designed for lives of ease and tranquility - for boredom. We were designed to meet challenges, not for boredom. This is true for all of humankind, but most particularly it is true for entrepreneurs. Boredom is a killer. The way to really come alive is to accept life's challenges. Meet those challenges with thought and action. That's what you do because you are an entrepreneur.

Now is a good time to begin to focus your thoughts on an overall plan, for until you do so, you cannot win big! With a long term plan you can become the person of your dreams. Others will immediately sense this. Just as people are fascinated by a speeding train roaring through the crossing in front of their idled cars, people will be fascinated by the progress being made by another powerful object - you - as it moves vigorously toward a definite objective. As a powerful locomotive does, you can pull many others along the tracks with you. So, focus your thoughts on that overall, long term plan. You have to be sure that the tracks will take you straight to your objective.

Step Two: Consider The End From The Beginning

"Advance, and never halt, for advancing is perfection."
Khalil Gibran

There is a painting of a pioneer family looking down on a caravan of wagons from atop a nearby bluff. The wagon train was having a difficult time of it as it wound along the dusty, rock-strewn trail. The family, a tall, rugged man, his gaunt wife, and their two children, one held in the wife's arms and the other holding onto her hand, had facial expressions that left no doubt as to the many difficulties they had overcome to get that far. From the look of things, they had a long way to travel still. At the bottom of the painting was an inscription I will never forget. It read: "The cowards never started and the weak died along the way."

Did those pioneers dwell on the difficulties they would be facing before they began their westward journeys? Certainly they would have given it some thought, and they no doubt discussed it with their families. Yet, despite odds that you and I might consider to be overwhelming, those pioneers went forward and settled the West. It is interesting that boredom and unhappiness were two of the main motives for their westward migration. In the dreary settlements along the East Coast, people had a lot about which to be unhappy. Had they not been the type of people who could pick up and follow their dreams, they might never have started. Perhaps they knew that their personal dreams might not be realized, but they also knew that if someone didn't begin the move, their children and grandchildren would be doomed to lead the same dreary lives that they found themselves to be living. So they set out on what became one of the greatest positive migrations in history.

The pioneers were able to overcome the difficulties that confronted them because they had an overriding purpose for their lives. They were carving out new farms and new lives for future generations. Without purpose in life a person becomes almost depraved. Without a purpose a person is not much different from the beasts. Since most people must spend the majority of their waking hours working to provide life's essentials, they seldom spend much time thinking about the reasons for which they exist. As an entrepreneur, you have a duty to discover your purpose for being here. The search is not necessarily easy, and your findings may change from time to time. Even so, you have an obligation to think about your reason for living. What is it that you intend to accomplish in this life? What would you like to see written on your tombstone?

Once you answer that question you will find it much easier to guide your daily actions into an overall, more rational framework - all of which works to accomplish your life plan. You have to be able to see if the castles you are building in air really fit into the ground-level situation in which you live. As you build on your dream from day to day, it is important to keep your long range plan clearly in mind. Your long range goal should be more than just a physical thing, such as a certain sum of money or a high standard of living. It is important that you concentrate on what your personal condition will be when you reach your long range objective. There will be a time when you will no longer be walking on this earth. What will you leave behind of which you can be proud? For what will you be remembered?

I once heard someone remark that it would be nice to have been born with the inner wisdom possessed by Abraham Lincoln. When I heard that, I had to laugh. Does anyone actually believe that Lincoln was *born* great? No, Lincoln had to grow into greatness. So, right now, you have no good way by which to know for what you will be remembered. If you ask yourself, almost on a daily basis, what it is that you are really trying to accomplish in life, a close approximation of the answer may eventually be revealed to you. Lincoln had to spend thousands of hours studying and thinking in order that he might arrive at his personal philosophy of life. You, too, may have to spend years in relative obscurity, denying yourself the easy pleasures that deter you from greatness in order to one day reach the heights of which you are capable. You should learn how to be content with small things and small victories. If you cannot do this, you may never be content with anything. Take pleasure in those few minutes spent thinking about who you are and where you are going.

Those may turn out to be the most valuable minutes of your life.

When some people think about their long term goals they may focus only on being considered to be a great success by all who know them. Such people are going to be failures! Instead, you should aim for achievement and for pleasing yourself. If your attempt is strictly to become famous, you will experience a life of frustration - for you will never become well enough known to be satisfied. By trying to please yourself and by aiming for achievement you can be a true success and become very well known if it suits you.

But don't let money become your driving force. Your objective should not be to get ahead of other people, but rather to get ahead of yourself.

As an entrepreneur you may even have to make your life a mission in itself, not just a series of disconnected trips. You have to work out your personal philosophy and your life plan. Don't be like the wanderers who drift from one town to another with no real purpose other than to rest up before moving on to yet another town. Don't let your life be like that saying that I saw written under the picture of an old Merry-Go-Round?

> *"Ride, ride the carousel, and reach for the golden ring.*
> *Never to finish, but to begin again, life is a circular thing.*

Remember, wherever you see a straight line, you can be sure that a determined human being has been there. Are you riding the carousel, or are you leaving a straight line behind you?

After you have considered your overall purpose, you can proceed with an easy mind along your daily path. No longer will you have to worry about whether or not you will lead a successful life. Now you need mostly to concern yourself with having today be a successful day. You may, from time to time, become discontent and feel that your progress is too slow, but don't worry about that. It won't be easy for you to keep on striving to make this planet livable for future generations, but with a bright, shining purpose in sight you will find that you will enjoy the work that much more. It is a continual climb, and if you don't enjoy the climbing, you will discover that getting to the top isn't worth what it took to get there.

Success is certainly a journey - not a destination. You are not likely to ever really reach your distant objective because you will most likely find that it is a constantly moving target. However, if you will take the time to notice what it is that you have already done, you will be provided great pleasure. I do not yet live in the house of my dreams, and I may never. Whenever I move into a new dwelling I am already planning on where I will go from there. Yet, I do enjoy walking around my current home and seeing the things I now have - without bothering to think about the things I still want. When it rains I take great pleasure in my non-dream house, for without it I would likely be very wet and cold. Does that sound corny? Well, it's the truth. No matter how successful we become, human nature directs us to want still more. Appreciate what you already have, and understand that your success will be measured by the distance you have traveled from where you started. You are on a great journey. Don't take that journey without a map. Begin today to think about where your life is really taking you.

Step Three: Are You Sure Your Dream Is Big Enough?

"Make no little plans. They have no magic to stir men's blood."
Daniel H. Burnham

Star Trek, one of the more popular of all television shows, always opened with a statement regarding the mission of the Starship Enterprise. The statement ended with the admonition "to boldly go where no one has gone before."

In Part One you were advised to be sure to dream a BIG dream so that it might help you through the difficult times that lie ahead. As in Star Trek, the grander the scheme - the bolder the step - the easier it is to get people to follow you, as strange as that may seem.

So let's pause for a moment and explore the characteristics of a big dream. For some people, opening a six-table restaurant might be a big dream. Someone else might consider a big dream to involve working out of their home as an interior designer. Others may dream of founding a multi-thousand employee company with offices around the world. All of those are big dreams as long as they involve more than the dreamer thinks he or she can actually achieve. To qualify as a truly great dream, the dream must stretch the dreamer's belief to its very limits. When viewed from a distance, most mountains appear to be impassable, but from close up and from their tops we often find that the mountains we have climbed are not really that high after all. When you look at the next mountain from the top of the one on which you are standing, it doesn't look all that high either - but you have to climb that first mountain to get the true picture.

Right now you are still doing the initial thinking about your new enterprise. You have not committed yourself to any particular path, so keep your mind free of all constraints. You will find that this type of mental activity becomes very easy, simply because you need not take the default reality into account. Now is the time to let your mind really run wild. If you think small, you will remain small. Later on you will be forced to compromise with reality, but now is the time to let the wheels run free.

As you sort out your big dream, strange things will happen to you. You will find that you actually begin to look forward to getting up each morning, now that each day is a new day during which you can work on your future. You may still have your old job and duties to perform, but you can anticipate the enjoyment of refining your new ideas. Each new day is a day of *your* life, not a day of someone else's life in which you are just playing an incidental role. Each day is a day that belongs to you. So, stretch that day by stretching your dreams. By reaching for heights that you cannot yet touch you will improve your ability to reach for them. As a result, you will become better prepared to design the plans that will turn your dreams into realities.

My personal belief is that it is much better to attempt to do something great with your own business and fail than it is to attempt to do nothing and succeed. As an entrepreneur you are a dreamer, but you are in excellent company. All great people have been dreamers of one sort or another. Dreamers consistently bite off more than they can chew - but then they go on to swallow and digest it anyway. You have what it takes and you know you do. For too long now you have been like the frog at the bottom of the well. Looking up, the frog's vision of the sky is only as large as the top of the well. It is now time for you to stop being like that frog, climb out of your well and change your perspective. The infinite universe awaits you.

Step Four: Time For An Attitude Check

"Belief creates the actual fact."
William James

One cannot study the subject of attitude very long without coming across the works of the great Harvard psychologist, William James. When he first published his findings on the workings of the successful mind there were many who doubted that his work was really grounded on proper scientific principles. Today we see that much work has since been done confirming James' earlier studies. There can be little doubt about his correctness. James was the first to state that the true wonder of human beings was that they are the only creatures who can significantly alter their lives simply by altering their attitudes. How is your attitude today?

The Art of Becoming An Entrepreneur

When you think of high adventure, images of mountain climbers, jungle explorers, and sea captains often appear. Yet the greatest adventure of all is the growth of a human mind, an adventure too often neglected. Simply by changing your thoughts you can change your entire world. Your life is no more and no less than what your thoughts make it to be. Are you constantly short of money? Do you get several colds every winter? Is your job a boring dead end? If so, believe it or not, the problem is first and foremost in your own mind.

Wouldn't it be great to go back to the days of early childhood when we believed everything we were told. Tell a four year old that there are elephants outside, and the child will run to look. Mention to a child that Santa Claus likes cookies and milk, and on Christmas Eve there will be cookies and milk left out for Santa. Do you still believe in Santa? I do, and every Christmas morning there is at least one present under the tree for me from "Santa." In medieval times there was a great demand for alchemists who might turn lead into gold. Alchemy, as it turns out, isn't just a myth. A proper attitude, coupled with action, can turn anyone and anything into gold. Maybe you have already produced a lot of action - but what about your attitude? Attitude is the key.

Negative Nate is a good friend of mine. He is one of the hardest working of my friends. He is also adept at dreaming. But Negative Nate has one fatal flaw. He sees all the problems associated with his new ideas before he sees the possibility of success. Nate has actually gone into business on his own several times, and he always did very well in the beginning, while his idea was still fresh. Nate's downfall, however, is that he ceases to innovate and expand after a short while because every new idea he comes up with seems to him to have too many problems associated with it. Steer clear of Negative Nates. They are idea killers. Also, be careful to not become a Negative Nate yourself. If you believe that you cannot do something, your belief will likely come true. If you believe the impossible to be possible, then you can do impossible things. If you believe the possible to be impossible, well then, it will be impossible!

Years ago a friend told me that nothing was impossible. Feeling smart, I asked, "Have you ever tried to put toothpaste back into the tube?" Without saying a word my friend got a tube of toothpaste, squeezed out about an inch-worth of the paste, and then held a lighted match under the tube. That inch of toothpaste was drawn back into the tube. From that day forward I knew that nothing was impossible.

Hopefully you will never reach the point in your life when you feel that you have arrived. I have personally gone through two periods in my life when I had that feeling. Let me warn you. The closest thing to *arriving* is death. Look at it this way: what is there left for a person to do once he or she has arrived? No, it is not arriving we should strive for, but *becoming*. Don't focus only on finding happiness, and, conversely, don't fear unhappiness either. Believe that there will be periods of happiness and of unhappiness, both of which you should accept without your having to spend time and energy searching for either of them. Use your time to search for the *you* that has been locked inside all too long. It is time to free your mind to do its real work - thinking. This is the beginning of your new life, your life as an entrepreneur. Don't bog down your new life with the same old heavy attitudes that have held you down for so long a time.

Deep down inside of you there is a great person waiting to get out. It is not unusual for a person, when they are young, to believe that they are so special that they have been sent to this planet for a reason greater than just existing. Unfortunately most of us lose that special feeling as we grow older. It is time to recapture that sense of importance. You are special, and you came here for a special reason. It is now time to get on with it. Whatever you have done or become in the past, good or bad, is over. You can be forgiven anything except for not rising to the greatness that is within you. Have the courage of that which you hold deep inside. You were not born to be a me-too person. It is time for you to stand up and be counted. You have a great soul and, because of that, you have your own will. Until now you may have avoided paying the price that will be asked of you. That doesn't mean that you can continue to avoid becoming what you were meant to be.

It is the time for you to set your attitude in tune with that which you were meant to be. Your purpose in this life is not to merely exist. Your purpose is to LIVE! Don't waste your days by simply prolonging them; instead use your time to build the life you were meant to live. You are a winner and it is time you realized that. Why else would you be starting your own business? You have chosen to join the ranks of those who set the pace for the human race. You are an entrepreneur. You must go boldly where no person has gone before.

Step Five: Take A Look At The Risks

"The desire for safety stands against every great and noble enterprise."
Tacitus

One of my favorite songs is by Kris Kristofferson and is titled, "Risky Business." Here are a few of the words: "...I'm afraid we've gone and laid it on the line. It's a risky business. ... While they gamble in your corner, boy, you rolled ... but the best that you can do is buy some time 'til they can find somebody better. ... It don't matter what they call you when you know you've been the best that you can be."

There is certainly an amount of cynicism in those words, but they will do nicely to help carry you through the lonely hours you will spend agonizing over the chances you are about to take. No matter what it is that you intend to do, there are going to be other people whose lives will become wrapped up in what you are starting. Since every entrepreneur I know is the type of person who has concern for others, it seems fair to generalize that persons who have what it takes to become entrepreneurs will be concerned for those others who become involved in the projects. What, then, are your responsibilities towards those people? Simply this - do your very best by them. Do not intentionally hurt anyone. That's it! You have no further responsibilities.

There are many people who will gamble in your corner in one way or another. They are doing it because they believe that the risk they are taking is more than justified by their faith in you. Your job is to roll the dice. Those who gamble in your corner know their risks better than you do. So don't kid yourself that they do it because they want to help you or feel sorry for you. They are putting their time and money on the line because they want to win, and they believe that you have a better chance than they do in coming up with a winning number.

Taking a calculated risk is a great thrill, yet once a person reaches maturity, it seems that one's risk-taking potential begins to diminish. During the early stages of idea formation there is the danger that a potential entrepreneur might not actually go ahead and take the risk needed to get the business going. In the next part of this book, "Nuts and Bolts," I will explain how you might keep your risk to such a minimum that you will never again be afraid to venture forth with a new business plan. For now, though, you must continue to forge through with your idea despite the fact that there is risk involved.

Why are people afraid to take even small risks in order to make dreams of having their own businesses come true? Many would say that it is the fear of losing their money, or worse yet, losing everything they have thus far acquired. Those fears may be present, but I believe that the real fear is the fear of failing - of losing face. It is easy to take risks when there is little or nothing to lose. This is particularly true when it comes to the possibility of loss of status. It is amazing how many people there are who have absolutely no fear of losing money, but who are terrified at the thought of going out on their own and not making it.

If you have lost some of your former adventure-seeking

spirit and are beginning to long more for comfort and security, and if you concentrate only on holding what you have - beware. You are experiencing the first signs of mental aging and decay. This aging and decay can happen at almost any age. I know people who are in their twenties who are mentally old, and I know some people in their eighties who are just now beginning a new venture. If you feel the signs of mental aging coming on, don't yield to the process. It is a daring spirit that keeps people young and vibrant. Taking a chance is a sure sign of youth, for it is only the young at heart who are willing to be daring. The older *at heart* a person is, the more careful he or she tends to be.

By taking a chance and starting a new business you are declaring your intention to continue building your life. You are setting the world on notice that you are not yet done with living - that there are great things for you yet to come. Don't worry that some find fault with what you are doing. If you do only the things with which others can't find fault, then there is little left for you to enjoy doing. You must have the courage to bet on your own idea. You must have the courage to take those calculated risks and to act. Sure, you might fail and have to begin again. It is still much better to attempt something and to fail than it is to attempt nothing and succeed.

Step Six: Remember, This Is Your Song

"Live for yourself, live for life, then you are truly a friend of man."
Kahili Gibran

The Art of Becoming An Entrepreneur

Anyone who has considered entering upon the life of the entrepreneur has undergone much self doubt. This includes Edison, Ford, Carnegie - all of them. You don't often read about the trying times experienced by these people. Their successes make much more exciting reading. But, late at night, all alone, when everything seemed to be crashing around them, they had their moments of doubt. However, these were individuals who would not let years of negative conditioning beat them. For you to overcome the repressive teaching you have had in the past, you must begin today to restore yourself to be the kind of person you were as a child. You have a right to be you!

Becoming an entrepreneur involves much more than simply starting one's own business. The entrepreneur must take charge of his or her own life as well as take charge of a business. Being in charge, you will no longer be able to blame outsiders and outside forces for any failures and unhappiness. From the moment you decide to take charge, whatever is to be is entirely up to you. The responsibility is increased by the fact that everything and everybody involved with you depend upon you. This is a heavy responsibility, but a joyous way to live.

Thoreau claimed that most men lead lives of quiet desperation. Are you quietly desperate? If so, how did you get that way? Dreamers are not desperate. Maybe it all began with your first credit card. What a disaster! With that card you went into hock to your own image of yourself. How does that image now appear to you? Maybe it's time to change. We are given so few years in which to accomplish that which we must do. So don't waste time on the unimportant things when you should be building the life you were born to live. Life is too brief, but it need not be too small. Live large!

Visiting with men and women who served in the armed forces during a war has always intrigued me. For many of those veterans, their war was the greatest adventure of their lives. Think of that! The high point of their lives was when they were forced to leave their homes, enter the military, and fight a war. That is a depressing thought. Although many of these veterans are now successful people, they still think of their war years as having been the most exciting times of their lives. Those veterans could have become entrepreneurs had they taken charge of their own lives instead of submitting to the government taking charge for them. What a fine world they could have built. Now, however, many of them are bored, leading comfortable lives to be sure, but longing for those grim war days when they were poor, dirty, and yet fully alive in some unnameable way.

A general once told Napoleon that a new campaign was unthinkable. He reported that the men were weary of war. They would not be willing to fight again. Napoleon replied, "Wrong! They will fight. I will be rescuing them from the button factories."

For generations we have been searching for the peaceful equivalent of war. Entrepreneurs understand that it has been found. It is simply to struggle to become our own person and to not give in to the demands of conformity that lesser minds want to place upon us. More entrepreneurs are needed to join the fight. I truly believe that we exist for the achievement of our positive desires. It is therefore difficult for me to understand by what right anyone else can demand that you waste a single hour of your life. Why are you still in the button factory when you have a duty to yourself to sing your own song.

What is it that today binds you to a less than joyful life? We know what we *have* become, but we no longer understand what we *may yet* become. When we were younger, the future seemed boundless. We felt no threat of old age, no aches, no pains, no fear of failure. Then, one day we awakened to find that the dreams of youth were long ago, far away, and that the horizon no longer seemed to be as bright as once it did. If your youthful dreams are long ago and far away, if your horizon is dull, you have but one choice - you must drastically alter your course. Your maturity gives you some substance on which to build far better dreams than you could when you were too young to know much. You haven't lost your ability to dream and to enjoy success. You owe it to yourself to really live. You have to learn to ignore what you erroneously feel to be your duty and to stop doing what you think is expected of you. Instead, why not do what your dreams inspire you to do?

Being aware of the difference between what one is capable of becoming and what one really has become can be distressing. What will you answer if your Maker should ask you, "Why did you let your entire existence drift on by when, with a little effort, you could have lived life to the fullest?"

We really should teach our children to search for what it is that they want to do - need to do - to be successful in their own eyes. Failure is doing what we don't want to do.

71

Success is doing what we do want to do. So make your life a mission, not an intermission. Sing your own song!

Step Seven: Outline Your Preliminary Plan

"If one advances confidently in the direction of his dreams, and endeavors to live a life which he has imagined, he will meet with a success unexpected in common hours."
Thoreau

Many motivational speakers compare the act of going after a particular goal to the act of climbing a mountain. While the symbolic drama of mountain climbing is hard to escape, I like that metaphor for another reason. That reason is the fact that great mountain climbers, like my friend Peter Taylor, set out after particular, well-defined goals. Mountain climbers don't go around saying that they were just out walking around and happened to reach the top of a mountain.

Did you know that most people spend more time each year planning a two week vacation than they spend planning for the next five years of their lives? If that describes you then it is time for you to begin working on a specific plan for your future. Today is the best day to begin this. Postponement can only result in failure. People who get ahead in life are those with specific goals toward which they actually work. These successful people also stay flexible so as to be ready to take advantage of new opportunities that arise - opportunities that were not present when they began working toward their goals. A good way to begin is to lay out the framework for your new venture.

This will give you definite direction and yet leave you with all of the options you need to be able to move in ever more profitable directions.

By now you should have sorted through the options available to you, and you should also have established a long-range objective. Yet remember to remain flexible so that you can add to, or change, your choices of options and your long-range objective as your plans evolve. The important thing is to continue to refine your dreams *right now*.

From here on, you should read this book with paper and pencil at hand, and you should stop reading and take the action suggested at the time you read about it. Further, you are assumed to be working on a very big dream, that your head is screwed on straight and tightly, that you are prepared to deal with the limited risks involved at this point in time, and that you have decided that you aren't going to put this off any longer.

If these things are so, then you will be in business for yourself by the time you finish this book - and you will also have overcome any lack of money, any fear of failure, and any enterprise killers who happen to come along.

Now place before you the paper on which you wrote Step Ten as suggested in Part One. Look again at the central idea of your new venture. As you concentrate on that thought, write down as many things as you can think of that must take place prior to your receiving any income from that idea. Earlier, we discussed the example of earning a living while being involved with sail boating. We will continue on that same theme here.

In this example, we have now examined all of the options and let's say that we have decided to focus on establishing a monthly newsletter in which we will write about sailboat chartering. This, then, might be how our list would look:

STEPS AND EVENTS BEFORE FIRST INCOME

Name the newsletter
Get a mailing address for it
Make an outline of its contents
Establish the subscription price
Locate mailing lists
Open a bank account
Take care of all legal matters
Contact sailboat charter companies
Contact sailboat owners

As you can see, this list could quickly build up to several pages or more. The key is to describe each task on paper as a single line item and to not get bogged down in details at this time. Keep your new list near you - in the car, at the bedside, and nearby when at work. Many of your best thoughts spring up during the night or while doing other things.

Next to each of the items on the list, jot down the date on which you will begin that step. There is no point in setting completion dates, but you can surely set up beginning dates for each task that must be done before your new business can generate income. You will quickly notice that there are many items that can be started before you solve that possible money problem.

The first step and the third one in the example above can be done immediately. You might later select another name for the newsletter and you will undoubtedly change the contents, but you can begin to use a working title and have a rough idea of the contents at this time. You can also use your home address as the beginning business address, and you could select a ballpark subscription price based upon what you would be willing to pay for such a newsletter yourself. A low-cost or no-cost trip to the public library will result in your obtaining directions for locating suitable mailing lists, and you will be able to compare your own newsletter ideas with currently available publications. You will soon find that you won't require much money, if any, to accomplish most of the items on your list. In addition, as you begin more and more tasks, you will find that your excitement will begin to grow.

Guess what? You have just begun your new business! Think about that.

As you pursue each task on the list, you should insure that it is going to help you travel toward your long range goal. If you notice that one of the steps points you in the wrong direction, you will have to alter the task or alter your long range goal. Whenever this happens, don't drift. Make a decision.

Keep a personal calendar. Note the tasks to be started on the appropriate dates on the calendar. We are not going to get into personal time management discussions in this book, but it is of importance to understand that the chances for your success are slim unless you keep a personal calendar and a written daily work list. After many attempts, I found a system that suits me and that is effective 100 percent of the time. I carry a small 12-month calendar and a small notebook for my daily work list. You can buy these in pocket-size sets that come complete with a flexible cover. Use the two of them to assign the necessary daily tasks to yourself. If you have no system, too many days will go by with no action - and your idea will simply die.

Start off by allotting your time for the next several weeks during which you will work on your new business. Don't even wait to run on down to the store for that fancy calendar-notebook gadget. Grab up a piece of paper and a pencil and start writing dates and tasks. You will quickly understand that every date for which there is no listed task is a day on which nothing will get done. You might like to think of those days as days during which your business remains closed.

Now, be sure to get that calendar and the notebook. The Chinese have a proverb that says, *"The strongest memory is weaker than the palest ink.*

Be careful to be realistic about the things you write, but do start writing! Be realistic about the time allocations. If you prove yourself to be overly ambitious as to what you can do, time wise, you will soon find that your enthusiasm will diminish as you miss deadline after deadline. Don't try to be Superman or Wonder Woman. You cannot fly faster than a speeding bullet. The race you are in is a race with yourself as the only contestant. Just keep moving forward every day and you will win the race.

What should you do if you miss starting a task on the day you set for it to be started? The first thing to do is to not worry. Just do something every day to advance your way toward that long range goal. Perhaps you set up a date to discuss your business with the attorney. Some judge, outside of your knowledge, ordered him into court that day. Guess who didn't get to see the attorney that day. Don't worry. Reset the task to another date. You cannot be responsible for everything, but you *are responsible for you*.

Your daily work list will help keep you motivated. The list allows you to concentrate on your daily performance, and the outcome will be both better and very motivational.

Remember: "What you think is what you become."

Whatever it was that you were thinking six or more months ago is what you are today. If you are happy, excited about life, and prosperous, it is because those were the types of thoughts that you were then experiencing. If you now spend most of your time worrying about paying the bills, then you will likely be grim, unexcited, and broke in another six months or so. Your actual life and your dreams are not really the same, but it is not possible to live without dreaming - and your pleasant dreams will die if you aren't actually vibrantly alive.

That list of tasks close at hand will help get you started on building the foundation of your newest and most exciting dream. Keep the list with you. Add to it, think about it, and read it daily. It is the roadmap to a new and better life for you and your family.

Your list will solidify the first goals for your new venture. These goals may not seem like much, but they can be very powerful. Here is a dramatic example of the power of physically seeing one's goal before them. The story is about the great swimmer, Florence Chadwick. The first time she attempted to swim the treacherous channel between Catalina Island and the coast of California, Chadwick swam for fifteen hours and forty-five minutes. After all of that effort, she didn't make it to the coast. She was but a half mile away from the coast when she quit. The weather that day was foggy, and neither Chadwick nor the boat crew accompanying her had been able to see the coastline just several hundred yards away. Chadwick said later that, had she been able to see the coast, she could have reached it. Keep your goal and your task list on paper and in view. You become that about which you are thinking. Keep your list in front of you and you will become the person you want to become.

Step Eight: Begin Showing Your Idea To Others

"Some fellows dream of worthy accomplishments while others stay awake and do them."
Anonymous

The moment of truth is about to arrive for you and your new venture. It is now time to tell others about your idea. Until now, most of your effort has been spent on thinking and on accomplishing some of the fact-gathering tasks. If you have been making respectable progress, your list of tasks to be done is actually getting longer, rather than shorter, but you have gained insight into your business venture that you didn't have earlier .

Now that you are well prepared, you can begin to contact

other people useful to your venture with the thought of getting them to follow you. You really couldn't do this earlier, because you were groping still and not at all ready to be convincing about your serious intentions.

What do you tell those first people to whom you divulge your idea? What you tell each of them depends on what you want from them - what you want them to do. Are you seeking money, advice, support, or time? Now what do you tell them? Simply ask for what it is that you want from them. That is about as uncomplicated as it can be, isn't it, yet it is surprising how few people will ask, straight out, for what it is that they want. Just go ahead and ask for what you want, straight out.

Take out that original listing that you made in Step Ten, Part One. On it should be the names of people whom you think can help put your idea into motion. Select from that list the one person who you feel will be the most important to your venture once it is up and running. This person may not be the person most important to your getting things started, but he or she may be one and the same. The person on whom to concentrate now is the one on whom you will be depending once your business is a reality.

That person will need to have almost as much enthusiasm for your venture as you have - and for a very long period of time. If, when you explain your idea to that person, he or she isn't immediately as excited as you are, then you had better look for another key person. However, you may be surprised to hear your key person say, "You know, I had that idea myself just last year - and I would have done it myself had I been able to come up with the money!"

Up to now we haven't talked about money. You have taken it on faith that this book is going to explain to you how to get the money. You have to do the same thing when talking with your contacts. Say, "Don't worry about the money. I'm working on that, and I don't think that we'll have any problems there."

That's all the information you need provide to others right now. Believe me, your contacts don't want to worry about the money anyway! If they liked to worry about finding the money to start ventures, they would have started their own businesses last year! The difference between you and your contacts is that you are good about dreaming with your eyes wide open - and they are not.

What if the person you see as potentially *the* key person rejects your idea? Then BANG! It feels as if someone just shot a bullet into your beautiful new idea. However, instead of feeling as if you had been shot, perhaps it would be a good idea to pause for a moment and reflect upon what they just told you. Was what they said valid? Maybe you just didn't explain yourself properly. More likely, however, you have gotten the normal, negative reaction from someone who didn't think of the idea before you described it. It is very important that you do not go back to that person. Once you have received a negative reaction from a contact, don't re-approach them with your idea. Steer clear of them with your thoughts about the venture. Eventually you will locate all of the good people you will need to work with you, but, right now, you are the only person essential to your plan. You will find that, as time goes on, you will be approached by people who possess talents far beyond those possessed by your current circle of acquaintances.

For whom are you looking? You should try to find the one or two people who will be almost as enthusiastic about the new idea as you are. Enthusiasm is the key. If your contact doesn't show enthusiasm, go on to the next contact. Save your efforts in convincing others so that you will have the strength to convince the money people of the merits of your ideas.

Every time you eliminate a person from your list of contacts, make a note of what it was that caused you to believe you needed him or her on your team. This will help you fill the slots with new people having those characteristics. The main characteristic to look for now, however, is enthusiasm.

Later on you will be contacting accountants, lawyers, and possibly other financial advisers. Their attitudes will likely shock you. From them you will learn of all of the many things that can go wrong. They will try to convince you to give up on this wild idea of yours. Here you are, doing that which makes the world a little better, building a new enterprise that will create new jobs, and yet these merchants of fear are asking you to pay them their professional fees to try to kill your idea. Be sure to arrange a meeting with one or more excited people to follow a session with these professionals. You will definitely need a pick up. Try to keep in mind that these attorneys, accounts, and the like are to be considered as mechanics. You should tell them what it is that you want done, and they should do it. If what you want done doesn't get done, get yourself another mechanic.

So here is where we are right now. You have taken your

original idea and have massaged it into an overall plan for living a happy, productive life. You nave begun the first steps toward the opening of the doors of your business, and you have started to tell others that you are up to something new. What next? Here comes the real fun for you, because from now on no one can deny the fact that you *are* an entrepreneur.

Summary of Part Two: Refining Your Idea

1. List all possible options

2. Establish an overall objective

3. Keep your head on tightly and straight

4. The only risk is in not going forward

5. Sing your own song

6. List the initial steps and assign to each a starting date

7. You will become what you think about

8. Discuss your plans with those most important to the venture

Part Three – Nuts and Bolts

Learning How To Fly High

September 5th.

I did it! Today I piloted the balloon from its takeoff to its landing. High winds two days earlier had prevented my first piloting - you cannot launch a hot air balloon in a gale! That had been a great disappointment, for I had stayed awake almost the whole of the night before in anticipation. Today more than made up for that.

Four other balloons took off at the same time we did, but my balloon was the prettiest of them all. My flying wasn't all that pretty! I didn't do too well at level flight. Every time I saw treetops approaching I overburned and the balloon shot up like a yo-yo.

I may not be a smooth pilot yet, but I'm on my way. Tomorrow I will have another lesson. I must work on level flight!

Formalizing The plan

"Things may come to those who wait, but only the things left by those who hustle."
Abraham Lincoln

You have now reached the point where being an entrepreneur gets to be fun. Until now you have had to deal with the torment of making your decision to actually begin. The reason for writing down all of your options and all of those initial steps was that doing so is about the only way there is to come to a decision and to go forward with a business idea. The initial decision-making period is so difficult that most people never get past it. As a result, they spend the rest of their lives playing the game of IF-IDA... "If I'da done this or if I'da done that..." By getting your idea onto paper you were able to break through that barrier and arrive right here. From now on there is to be no going back. You are an entrepreneur, so get on with your project.

Whenever I give a seminar on the "nuts and bolts" of a business plan I find that the audience tends to expect advice on how to manage the day-to-day affairs of a business. While I will not deny the importance of knowing how to structure daily operations, the "Nuts and Bolts" for an entrepreneur demand more than do the day to day operations. Your responsibilities include the overall planning and execution of your entire operation, much more than simply overseeing the routine things. You have to concern yourself with all of the parts of the overall business plan of the enterprise. That's a lot of "Nuts and

Bolts."

It may surprise you to learn that those gentle giants floating in the sky, those hot air balloons, need a lot of piloting. Just as that might amaze you, I am all too often amazed at how many people think that they can open up a new business and have it float in the air of commerce without the piloting guide of a long range, formal business plan. That is why this section is included in this book. Using it as a framework, you can develop a plan for any business, from a small, in-home operation to a multimillion dollar corporation. All successful business have the same major ingredients which must be properly combined using a recipe - a plan of action. Success will not come to you of its own accord. You must make it happen. You need to begin your business with a formal, three-year plan. Success can be organized, but you have to have a formal business plan in order to do this.

There are many ways to work up formal business plans. The method that I will explain here is one that I use in my own businesses. It works. You can certainly modify my method to fit your particular style and your particular venture, but the outline that I give you here may be used if you have never prepared a business plan before.

The Business Plan

Organize the physical aspects of the plan. Divide it into various parts. This makes it easier for you and others to review it. This also forces you to concentrate on each element of the business so that the complexity of the whole will not overwhelm you. After your business plan is written, print it and place the pages in a three-ring binder with plastic tabs to separate each section of the plan from the next one. This will also help you create a mind-set that will keep you acting professionally and well organized throughout the duration of your business.

Here is the format I use:

1. Guidance Statement

2. Specific Objectives

3. Marketing Strategies

4. Financial Plan

5. Manpower

6. Internal Operations

7. Financial Statements (if applicable)

Later, we will deal with each of these sections in detail. At that time we will explore various ways to use the plan to determine cash needs and to assist you in raising necessary capital.

Several of my entrepreneur friends claim that formal business plans are a waste of time. They say that they can spend that time more profitably by actually starting the operations of the company. What they fail to realize is that writing the business plan IS starting the company. To begin a business venture without a written plan is worse than driving across the country without a road map. It can be done, but you can spare yourself much time and a lot of grief if you use a good map - and a good plan.

Do you remember when seat belts were first installed in cars? At that time they just hung loose when not fastened and, often, they fell out onto the ground through an open door and dragged along the ground when the car moved. To solve that problem I purchased a kit that consisted of a small cylinder for each belt and one metal spring per cylinder. These gadgets were to work together to roll up the seat belts when the belts were not in use. I opened the package, tossed the direction sheet to one side, and went to work. Nothing to it! I wound the first spring, slipped the cylinder onto a seat belt, let go... and the thing went wild, spinning around and beating the devil out of my thumb. So I tried again. And again. And again. After about an hour of trying, I picked up the direction sheet, read the instructions and came upon instruction number three. I will never forget it. It read, "Once the spring has been wound, place locking bar C in slot D and slip onto seat belt."

So, I followed the instructions, and guess what? They worked. By use of the written instructions it took me but ten minutes to install all four units - without beating the devil out of my thumbs!

You have a choice. Beat the devil out of your thumbs or write down the instructions that you will be needing when your business' springs begin to unwind. You see, the business plan has two purposes: 1) It forces you to prepare an organized plan of attack and 2) It will help keep you on track as your business develops. For your business plan to have value to you, it must be a living document - you have to refer to it and use it often. In fact, you should make a note to yourself right now: RE-READ YOUR BUSINESS PLAN AT LEAST ONCE A MONTH! It is amazing how some large corporations devote thousands of expensive person hours working up business plans which, once completed, are put up on the shelves until next year. Your business plan is to be your road map. You need to consult it regularly. A well-organized entrepreneur will set aside one day each month on which to review the business plan.

Begin your actual business operations only after you have completed your business plan - even if the form is still only a rough draft. To paraphrase Vince Lombardi, "Once you have a plan, the rest is simply a matter of execution!"

Section 1 – The Guidance Statement

Just what is a guidance statement? It is simply a statement of the overall policies of a business. The guidance statement deals with the big picture, making broad, sweeping statements as to what your business is and where it is heading.

Here is humorist Will Roger's guidance statement for getting rid of the German submarine threat during World War I: "Raise the temperature of the ocean to 212 degrees Fahrenheit. Once it gets hot enough, the subs will surface, and we can pick 'em off one by one. "

When asked how he intended to warm up the ocean, he replied, "That's a matter of detail, and I'm a policy maker!"

You, too, are a policy maker - at least insofar as your guidance statement is concerned. Don't get too carried away with Will Roger's example, though, for the next section of your plan must take those grand policies and add details that can bring them into existence and make them work. Don't come completely back to earth, however. Your overall plan should be a grand one. Big ideas call for big plans. Get into the proper frame of mind as you settle down to work out your guidance statement. For example, take a large piece of paper -maybe one that is 24 x 36 inches in dimension. Jot a small, black dot right in the middle of the sheet. Then back off several feet and ask yourself what it is that you see. Most people will say that they see a black dot. An entrepreneur will see a very large sheet of paper. Look first at the big picture. Later on there will be ample time to look for black dots.

To make writing the guidance statement easier, break it down into four categories: **MISSION, GOALS, OBJECTIVES, and STRATEGIES.**

Of the four, the mission is by far the hardest to define.

One of my friends was chairman of a 600 million dollar international corporation. Each year the company officers would spend thousands of person-hours to write a business plan covering the next fiscal year. As soon as the plan was completed and approved, it was put away in a file. Next year they would take up the old plan and see how they did in comparison with what they had planned to do. What a waste of time. My friend decided to do something about this. He interviewed everyone involved with the business plan project. He asked each of them, "What is the mission of this corporation?"

He had as many different answers as there were people interviewed. What he did next impresses me still. He took the top seven executives of the corporation and sequestered them, along with himself, in a hotel. He left strict instructions behind that there be no communication with his group until they agreed upon a mission statement for the company. They worked four days, around the clock, and finally arrived at a two-sentence mission statement on which all agreed on every word.

Some may feel that these people simply took a four day vacation, but, looking at the company's results from that time forward, it is obvious that something dramatic happened at that hotel. What had been developed was one simple guideline from which to direct the company's growth. From then on it became simpler to decide on whether or not to add some new production equipment, to acquire another business, or to do the many other things companies must do to grow. All that had to be done now was to review the mission statement and to see if the new opportunity fit into the picture they had created. As your own business grows, you will have more and more opportunities to diversify and expand. Without a mission statement as your reference, you may wind up diversifying yourself out of business!

It should take you not more than two sentences to define

your company's exact mission - the specific goal with which your company is charged to achieve. It isn't all that easy to boil things down into a sentence or two, but the time and effort you spend on this will pay for itself many times over during the years ahead. Read your mission statement and re-read it. Stay within its boundaries.

Let's go back to that company that is to produce the sailboat chartering newsletter. Here might be its mission statement:

MISSION

The mission of Charter Boating Newsletters is:

> *To consolidate into one publication all the sources, prices, requirements, and options available to people who wish to charter sailboats; and to bring this information directly into their homes.*

Suppose that the following potential diversions came along. What decision would you make about each in light of the mission statement, above?

- People who sell charter services might ask you to direct editorial content at them and at their interests .

- You have the opportunity to carry paid advertising and editorial information regarding power boats.

- You have been offered the opportunity to open a store and to conduct a public seminar.

- A famous artist offers to let you run reproductions of his sailboat paintings as centerfolds in return for your providing him with free space for his own advertising.

- A sail boating magazine is folding and you can acquire it

at low cost.

Obviously, the answers to the above question depend upon you, the entrepreneur. And this is where the 'art' of being an entrepreneur comes in, for there is never a single correct answer to the many directions available in the early days of a new enterprise. Those decisions are up to you and you alone.

However, your mission statement will be a big help in making decisions like those you would have to make above. No mission statement can foresee all possibilities, but you need to have one that can at least carry you through the first two or so years. If it misses more often than it hits, you should probably sit down and re-think it.

Once you have settled on your mission statement you can move along to listing the overall goals of your new business. Don't confuse goals with the mission. The mission charges the company with its overall objective. The goals of a company deal more with the results that will be gained when, the mission is carried out.

A good definition of a goal is: "A point toward which effort is directed.

Remember that success is a journey, not a destination. Thus, your goals should be visible from a distance, and you should always have goals which remain at a distance. If you reach one goal, replace it with another, distant goal. Thus, you can see that the goal section of your business plan is and will remain dynamic. This is unlike the mission statement which should be cast in bronze or in concrete. Here is an example:

GOALS

The goals of Charter Boating Newsletters are:

To achieve above average growth in subscription rates with financial results equal to or surpassing those of the newsletter industry in general.

To be at the forefront of supplying knowledge of the sailboat chartering business to prospective customers and to increase customer loyalty and subscription renewals by supplying more information for less money than our customers could get elsewhere.

As you can see, those goals are very broad statements that point to where the business should be headed. This newsletter company is obviously considering becoming a leading supplier of information concerning sailboat chartering. To do this, quality information not readily found elsewhere is to be supplied to the subscribers. The profit for doing this should be above average for newsletters. Thus, the goals are points toward which immediate efforts are to be directed. The goals may at first seem to be too broad, but they are sufficient if they are understandable, seemingly attainable, and highly visible. You will bring them into better focus in the objectives section which follows.

Objectives are actually short-term goals. They are stepping stones along the way toward the long-term goals. Objectives are listed in the guidance statement for purposes of giving you a look at the immediate, the short-term, direction of the company. For example, the listing of objectives of the hypothetical newsletter company might read like this:

OBJECTIVES

The major objectives of Charter Boating Newsletters are:

To Increase the number of new subscribers 10 percent monthly during the first 24 months of business.

To achieve breakeven status by the end of the 10th month, and to have an operating profit, pre-tax, of 13% by the end of the 18th month."

Although the above example uses deadlines such as "the end of the 10th month" it is important to assign actual dates to deadlines. This will help prevent your falling into a "let it slide" sort of trap that might come along to kill an otherwise excellent business plan.

Finally, you should come up with a strategy section for the business plan. What is needed here is a concise statement or two of how you intend to achieve your various goals and objectives. The strategy section of the guidance statement is the place for you to state your key business philosophy, the one separating your company from its competition. Here is where you state what it is about your company that will cause your potential customers to leave their money with you, rather than with someone else. For example, if you are in the furniture selling business, is your price, your design, your utility, or your quality the main feature you will stress? How do you intend to stay ahead of the competition?

The simplest strategy is often the most effective. Here is one example of effective strategy. How do you get a child to take medicine? You can yell, threaten, and cajole all you want – yet, the candy-flavored, chewable pill will likely remain unswallowed. But leave the pill on the floor of the playpen and, soon, the youngster will pick it up and put it in his or her mouth. A good business strategy should be as simple as that.

Here is how the sailboat newsletter company owner might look at strategy:

STRATEGIES

The major strategies of Charter Boating Newsletters are:

To concentrate sales efforts in the coastal states of the Southeast

To establish a name and quality image for Charter Boating Newsletters through news releases and through boat shows

To develop or acquire an exclusive mailing list of people who have either chartered in the past or who have inquired about chartering

To build a team of contributing authors whose name identity will help build the image of a quality newsletter

To establish a quick response system to reply to letters from subscribers

To establish outside sales channels for the

newsletter

To enhance circulation by conducting seminars about sailboat chartering.

Obviously, the list could go on. In fact, it is a good idea to list every strategy of which you might think. Then, as the plan matures, you can remove the less desirable strategies from your list. This is a good time for "brainstorming". You might just come up with the one strategy that will help put you on top.

Your guidance statement will and should take a great deal of time and mental effort to prepare, but if you properly prepare it you will find that the rest of the business plan is much easier. After you have written your guidance statement, don't put it off to one side. Read it and re-read it. It is the cornerstone of your business, and it must be able to withstand every conceivable attack in the days and years to come.

Section 2 – Specific Objectives

This is the section of your business plan that should be prepared as a rough draft when formulating the plan and then, when you have completed the financial sections, you should return to this section and finalize it. It is in this section that specific statements as to the growth and development of your business should be listed.

There are subsections in the specific objectives listing. These subsections will vary from business to business, but the more common are:

Specific Company Goals
Executive Objectives
Marketing Objectives
Sales Objectives
Product Development Objectives
Plus other objectives related directly to your
business

Perhaps the best way to explain the specific objectives
illustration is to return to our newsletter company and show
you their listing.

Specific Corporate Goals for Year 1, Year 2, and Year 3:

1. To begin publication with 100 subscribers

*While the number 100 may seem extremely ambitious, it is
intended that for two months prior to publication of the first
issue a mass mailing will be made describing the newsletter
and offering a 50% reduction in subscription price for
charter subscribers, to be guaranteed throughout the
subscriber's lifetime.*

*2. 185% growth in subscriptions during the first 12 months
of publication*

*This growth rate approximates 10% per month increase in
subscriptions. It will be accomplished by continuing to
offer reduced rate subscriptions through direct mail as well
as by offering existing subscribers incentives to help locate
new subscribers.*

*3. To achieve breakeven status by the 10th month of
publication*

This will be accomplished by continuing to operate from the owner's home and by using family help rather than hiring outside workers.

The list could be much longer, but the idea is to provide you with insight - not to provide you with a complete listing of specific goals of a fictitious company. It is sometimes useful to be far more specific in detail than has been shown here. For example, the newsletter's plan could have provided full descriptions of the direct mail offers, plus explanations of the exact incentives being considered as offers for current subscribers.

Include in this section a statement of anticipated gross profit margin by operating year, as well as the profit expectations both before and after taxes. If you are starting your business using a significant amount of capital, then you should estimate the return to investors by year. It is probable that you will only be able to estimate things for the first draft of your business plan - in fact, the first draft should be more a continuation of your dream than black and white reality. It will be time enough for you to be forced back into the real world when, later in the preparation of your business plan, you must set out the financial plan and work out a projected cash flow statement.

The entrepreneur owner of the newsletter company might feel that a 10% monthly increase in subscribers is a legitimate specific goal - until, when setting up the actual budget, it is discovered that 500 new subscribers per month must be found to sustain that growth rate. There will be such a month. To come up with 500 new subscribers,

25,000 mailing pieces must be sent out. The cost of preparing and making this mailing might be considered to be too high, and so the decision might be made to keep the growth rate to some more easily affordable amount. To see how to make the decision, the newsletter owner would refer to the guidance statement!

So, work up the specific goal listing in rough form and, when the financial planning has been completed, work out the details more fully. Use the financial planning section to bring your entire business plan into sharp focus and to insure that you are not going to actually set your foot down on a banana peel!

Next write out the executive objectives, those which will most concern you as chief executive officer. One way to describe executive objectives would be to call them POLICY objectives. Another way of looking at executive objectives is to consider them objectives that cannot handily be monitored by your accountants - you will have to monitor their progress yourself.

This is the domain of the chief executive officer, typically you! Here are some of the things you may want to cover in this portion of the specific objectives listing:

> Control of overhead and the size of the workforce
> Conscious development of long range planning
> Control over the selection of a physical plant
> Acquisition of other companies

Obviously, the size of this section will depend on how many items you deem to be within your exclusive domain. It is wise to keep the description of each item on the list down to one or just several sentences - and to include a completion (or do-it) date with each. Keep in mind that others will be reviewing your business plan, so be realistic about these dates so as not to risk de-motivating the rest of your staff (or your banker) by the fact that you were overly optimistic and, therefore, missed all of your projected dates by a country mile.

Next, we come to marketing objectives. Marketing concerns how you are to distribute your products and services, to whom they will be distributed, and how you intend to gain and keep customers. Marketing and selling are often confused, for they are kissing cousins at the very least. Selling is handing over what you have for what the customer is willing to hand over to you. Marketing is about finding and keeping the customer.

Some of the items on your specific marketing objectives listing might be:

> Expansion of the current product line
> Repackaging of current products
> Diversification into other product lines
> Advertising and direct mail sales literature
> Trade show attendance
> Sales contests

You can include any marketing idea that you may now have. Be sure to include a specific date on which each idea will be implemented. Once this subsection is completed it is extremely important to make a copy of it that you can have with you so that you can read it daily. Don't simply hand this list over to someone else to be accomplished. None of the grand plans you forge will come to pass unless you demand that the marketing tasks be completed the way you intend them to be completed.

Next, list the sales objectives for each of the three years of your plan. The problem here is to be optimistic and realistic at the same time. You have to make real pie out of that pie in the sky, so to speak. A friend of mine was once asked how the coming business year looked to him. He replied, "I'm cautiously over-optimistic!"

It is all right to be cautiously over-optimistic!

Here is a four step system for developing a sales forecast. The method works well:

1. Prepare a detailed, month-by-month, product-by-product sales projection for the first 12 months. Often, the first few months of a business will show no sales. As you forecast the monthly sales, ask yourself how you intend to bring in the dollars you are projecting. Next, look at the second 12-month period. Assume that the initial problems of starting the business have been solved and that your new company is now up and running. Finally, make your third-year projections using the percent growth figures you specified in your listing of goals. After reviewing your sales projections, it may be that you will want to re-write the goals. If that is so, do it.

2. In the next major section of the business plan, marketing strategy, sales projections must be analyzed even more extensively, for example, by territory. Once you complete that section, come back to these sales projections and make any necessary changes.

3. After you complete the marketing strategy section, you

will prepare a formal financial plan covering operating costs and projected profits or losses. After you complete the formal financial plan, you may want to come back and revise these sales projections, forcing them into reality.

4. Finally, return to the goals listing and be sure that your goals are consistent with all of the other financial information you have prepared.

Drafting and redrafting your sales goals is the only effective way to maintain the optimistic attitude required of you, the main salesperson for your venture, while at the same time imposing some realistic planning to go along with your dreams. When the sales projections have been prepared, write a short explanation of the more detailed monthly projections. This will help outsiders (i. e. investors) understand your numbers. Don't forget the fourth step, above, the return to your goal listing. A prospective investor will dismiss your plan most quickly should it contain inconsistent information.

Finally, there is the product development objectives listing to be done. Some companies may not need much in this section, but for other companies it may be the major section. (Include "services" in your concept of products, for some companies may have more services than they do physical products.) List the new products (and/or services) that you intend to introduce over the next three years of the plan. Give specific dates for the development of each product or service and for its introduction to the market. I have found it useful to include the following items for each new product or service described:

1. A brief description of the product or service

2. An explanation of why the company needs to offer this product or service

3. When and how the product or service is to be introduced

Now the second part of your business plan has been completed. There is much that still needs doing. Yet, you have already made it all this way through a difficult, sometimes stormy, effort. You have thought about and formalized the how and the why of your business. The part of your business plan that you have completed will help you to make the financial plan part become reality. Those numbers mean little and will not take you very far without the how and the why part behind you. What you have done already has set the stage for your business. Now, after all of this work, your new venture has at least a 50-50 chance of being born.

Section 3 - Marketing Strategy

Now is the time to focus on how to achieve your sales objectives. It is not possible to provide a short listing of how to achieve sales, for there are as many different ways to go about it as there are businesses and people. Here, though, are the several things that MUST appear in the marketing strategy section of any well-thought-out business plan. For specific details of marketing strategies for various industries and various products, check out some of the textbooks in your local schools, libraries, and trade associations.

First, identify your target market. To whom do you intend to sell your products and/or services? At first, this may seem obvious, but that is not always so. A famous example of the error in not identifying the market can be seen by looking at the railroads. They all believed that they were in the railroad business. That got all of them into a lot of fiscal trouble except for the railroad companies who, in time to save their hides, realized that they were actually in the *transportation* business! Next, look at IBM's introduction and ballyhoo of the small computer they called the "PC Jr." IBM (a master at manipulating the news media through "leaks") was able to cause a massive amount of news coverage and excitement prior to PC Jr.'s actual introduction. By the time the first PC Jr. appeared in a store, everyone tended to believe that THIS was the final statement in computers for the home and personal user market. So much for that. Sales were slow. Customers didn't go for the product. IBM redesigned both its new machine and the marketing of it. Before long it was withdrawn as a sales failure.

Many people believe that the reason for the "Peanut" (as PC Jr. was called) to not make the grade was its overpricing and its non-state-of-the-art makeup. I believe, however, that it failed due to the company's non-specific definition of the market. Was this a home computer, a personal computer, a spare business computer? A marketing manager might argue that PC Jr. was all of those, the customer would argue that he or she didn't need to purchase the features for one user that were not needed by him or her! A real marketing manager would know enough to target the intended customer and to concentrate all sales efforts in that direction. Narrowly define your target market!

Your marketing strategy should next address itself to the

geographic limits in which sales are planned. Even small "Mom and Pop" stores must consider their geographic sales areas. Are there enough customers in the targeted group present in the area - and willing to come to the company's sales location? In some businesses, sales are made at the customers' locations, so you have to consider the costs involved in putting the salespeople out into the field where the customers live.

You must also consider things such as customer support, product repairs, sales call costs, and the like. There is likely to be little point in establishing sales in areas where those sales will be unprofitable - so, if the costs outweigh the benefits, either don't establish the sales or stop selling in those unprofitable territories. The idea is to make some profit - not to lose money on your sales. If it isn't profitable, don't do it.

Other items that should be included in the marketing strategy section are sales aids and salesperson education. Someone must buy your products, and someone must sell them. Business IS sales. You need to think about these things early in your planning. How are you going to educate your salespeople about the products and/or services they will be selling? What sorts of brochures and product literature are you going to have? There is more. You have to match the quality (or lack of it) of the literature you intend to provide with the type of product or service. It would be wasteful to have a 4-color brochure made up to send out to potential customers for a ten cent item, but that may be a mandatory style to use if you are in the limited first edition leather-bound book business. There are inexpensive ways to present your customers with information and with sales messages. Use those if you can. Do you want to send your salespeople to Hawaii for a workshop, or can they be coached simply by their reading of a coherent manual right at home? Maybe your commission schedule will prompt some self-learning. Think about these things.

Section 4 - The Financial Plan

At last, we now have reached the section of the business plan where most unpracticed entrepreneurs begin. Perhaps the reason that so many people jump right on into things and prepare a pro-forma financial statement first is that they may believe the pro-forma to be all that is needed to tell whether or not the blood, sweat, tears, and money to be spent will really pay off. True, a pro-forma financial statement can help determine the "bottom line" - and that is the place everyone looks to see how rich they are going to get, but it really takes all of the other information you have assembled thus far to come up with a reasonably correct pro-forma.

In the business plan outline shown in the appendix, you will notice that the plan is divided into several parts, one of which is **Income And Cash Flow Projections**. You will recall that you have already shown the projected business income (back in the sales objectives listing), so half of your work on this is already done. Keep in mind that you may have to modify your original sales forecasts as a result of your work on the marketing strategy section. It would not be too unusual for there to be a need to revise them once again following your completion of the financial plan.

Separate your expenses into different areas, each of which can be thought of as a department or as a budget group. For example, if you are going to be a manufacturer and seller of products, the major areas, or departments, might look like these:

General administration
Sales and marketing
Product manufacturing
Warranty and customer service

The financial plan should contain brief outlines or summaries detailing the plan's organization, showing references to the sales projection portions of your overall business plan, and, as well, a cash requirements chart covering the details of required funding throughout the period of the plan. Following this series of outlines and summaries should come the income and cash flow projections. These, in turn, should be followed by detailed departmental budgets.

You should actually begin your work on the financial plan by constructing the departmental budgets. Some of the costs involved will be fixed. For those which float with sales and marketing, you can refer to the earlier parts of your overall business plan to come up with realistic numbers.

For example, the general administrative budget would typically include wages for administrative personnel, the general payroll tax and insurance cost burden, office supply expenses, office equipment, telephone, rent, non-payroll insurance, travel and entertainment, postage, interest expense, note repayments, and miscellaneous costs. Some of these expenses might fit better in another department, and, of course, that depends on the business. Also, this listing is not meant to be all-inclusive, so examine your business carefully and try to include all of the expenses for each department.

The idea here is not to try to make an accountant of you, but to let you come to grips with reality - and to exercise you, using real financial figures that you have developed throughout the course of building your business plan. If you understand how to construct a departmental budget, then your battle to live within the budget you have made is almost won!

In your budget for the sales and marketing department you may also list wages, payroll tax, insurance burdens, and supplies, *et cetera*. Also, you will have to consider sales literature, advertising, sales contests, training, and incentives. It is very useful to show for each item listed its dollar amount **and** its relationship to monthly sales amounts as a percent notation. Those percentage figures provide a very clear picture of what is going on both for both you and for your financial advisers.

While it is extremely important to prepare a careful, detailed departmental budget covering the first twelve month period, it can be a waste of time to devote too much energy to developing the monthly summaries for the second and third years. It is not that budgets become unimportant after the first twelve months, they are important. But conditions will change so much by then that the best you can hope for now is a reasonable guess of your needs covering the second two years of the plan. Budgets are very important, and you should review your budget each month that you are in business.

The usual way of making reasonable predictions about the budgets after the first year of the business is to use the percent of sales figures for the last quarter of the first year as the guide. After compensating for any extraordinary expenses, apply the percent of sales figures to the monthly sales projections. This should help you be realistic and the numbers can be useful in your overall planning. Be aware of the fact that some expenses will have ceilings. For example, if your percent of sales multiplied by the sales projections for April in year 3 calls for you to spend $11,292 for wastebaskets, you can understand that you have gone through a ceiling unless, of course, you are the marketer of wastebaskets.

Estimated expenses in excess of the total sales income for a month are not unusual in the early months of a new business. Deficits cannot go on too long, however. Deficits can last quite a bit longer in a business requiring intensive research and development, but it should be obvious that if all the money is gone, the business is going to be gone, too. If there is an unusually large cash flow brought about by early success, the absence of *real* profit may be hidden for awhile, but if you study your budget in light of your sales and income performances each month, a large, seemingly positive, cash flow won't mask the fact that you are actually losing money. While you are still in the planning stages of your business you can do a lot to prevent going broke that way.

Suppose you find that the deficits projected over the period of the business plan exceed the total amount of capital available, what remedies are there for you to apply? There are at least three:

Increase sales income
Reduce expenses
Obtain more investment capital

When the departmental budgets are completed in rough form it is time for a moment of truth. You should now consolidate the projected sales figures, the budget figures, and the variable expenses into a single pro-forma financial statement.

In such a combined pro-forma financial statement, I like to list the sales projections right along with the variable costs of sales (such as cost of the product, commissions, freight, and so on.) Then, when you subtract the cost totals from the sales totals for that period, the number which remains is the amount of money you have left over from sales to run the rest of your company and, if possible, to have some of the remainder left to you as profit. The difference between sales and variable costs of sales can be called the GROSS MARGIN. Suppose that the gross margin is negative; that is, your variable costs exceeded sales income for that period? You must make up the difference from your capital. As you will recall, your costs have been separated by department. Now it will be easy for you to see where the money comes from and where it goes. In this way, your pro-forma financial statement will provide a concise picture of the profit potential of your business, and will assist you in making that potential come true.

The pro-forma is not meant to be a true statement of

company income and expenses. It is a collection of projections and targets. The Internal Revenue Service need never get a copy of your pro-forma - but some bankers seem to enjoy them. If you have done your thinking well, your actual performance and your pro-forma financial statements may look a lot alike - but rarely is there an exact match.

After you have determined that all of your monthly gross margin projections have been made, you must deduct from these any other expenses, for example income taxes, state franchise taxes, and the like. The resulting figure is that of *net income* - and it is the net income that you use when you construct your chart of cash flow. This is the chart on which you will rely to alert you to any impending cash shortages. It is also the chart that you will use to determine the level of cash investment required to begin and to operate your business during its first three years.

The cash flow chart is easy enough to read. Assume a loss during each of the first six months. As each month comes along, you add the new loss to the old one. The resulting number is the cumulative net loss. If, after the sixth month, each month is projected to show a net profit, the cumulative net loss slowly disappears - and a cumulative net profit begins to come along. You can use your reading of the cash flow chart to predict how much investment you will need and how long it will be before you and your investors can breathe somewhat of a sigh of relief and smile again.

Take into account the fact that, as a new business, you may have difficulty in immediately establishing credit with some suppliers. This will have a dramatic impact on your cash flow. Some suppliers may want cash up front or put your orders on a cash-on-delivery basis. Don't take this as a personal insult. Learn a lesson from it.

No matter how much you want or need sales, sales are worthless if you never get paid for what you sell!

As you build your various projections you will find that you have to go back and forth from one budget to another, from sales projections to income statements to cash flow projections. There is a constant give and take needed to achieve dollar balances that are workable, and which result in projected profits. There are spreadsheet programs that work with most personal computers, and these can assist you in the give and take processes. In your profit projections, be sure to account for sufficient payments to be made to yourself. If you don't personally profit, there is no way in which you can accumulate the additional capital required to expand your business. Then, the only way you will have left for expansion via capital input is to go outside for the new capital (i.e. sell some of your business to others.)

Detailed financial plans are less than useful if you construct them and then stick them into a file drawer until next year's revision time comes along. This financial plan is a useful tool - useful provided you use it - and much more than just a pretty number story to be handed out to potential investors. It is a benchmark against which the company's month-by-month progress can be measured. There may be the need to adjust the financial plan on a regular monthly basis, but using your plan should significantly increase the chances of survival of your business. Your financial plan is your road map. Read it often so as to not get lost.

Section 5 - Manpower

Just because you now happen to be your entire workforce, don't think that it is all right to gloss over this section of your business plan. While you are still *it*, dream ahead to the day when your business has grown to the point where your employees are doing all of the things you don't like to do and where you are free to spend your time setting policy and charting new directions! Right now you have to rent the office, manage the production, direct the sales, take out the trash - and dream! Furthermore, if you intend to present your business plan to the venture capital market, the **Manpower Section** is the single most important section of the plan. Investors bet on people - not on paper plans.

You cannot continue to do everything yourself. You have to learn how to share responsibility and authority. To succeed after the first short while, you must quickly learn that you become less and less efficient if you try to do everything yourself. You must not even try to master all aspects of your business. As your business grows, you will be able to hire the specialists you will need, You should specialize in the area in which you are best - being an entrepreneur.

Mark Twain once said, "Never learn to do anything. If you don't learn, you'll always find someone else to do it for you."

That's exaggeration, to be sure, but it is pretty good advice. Dr. Robert Schuler told an audience once to never do anything if they could find someone else to do it as well or better. Businesses are really people, so plan to gather the best people you can find and let them add to your own skills and strengths - freeing you to have more time to think and plan.

Here is one way to write the manpower section of your business plan:

Prepare a brief description of your own background and those of the key members of your team. Keep these descriptions brief, but be sure to include enough detail in each to show that your group can capably execute your business plan. This is the key section to venture capitalists - so be brief but complete. Check the volume of business you have projected for the last quarter of the third year of your plan. Then, calculate and list the amount of time it will probably require to perform each task associated with achieving that volume. This can really get into details. For example, list how much time it will take a clerk to enter a sales order on the books, write out a packing slip, type the invoice and mail it to the customer. For that same order, figure out how much time the shipping department will take to get the order out the door. List the time required to select that product, to manufacture it, to deal with suppliers, to order it, to receive it, service the customers, keep employee records - even filling out all of the forms required of you by the government. Once you have estimated the time required for each task associated with receiving and processing an order, you will be in the position to determine how many people it will take to operate that part of the business at various levels of sales. From there, you can work out the structure of the company and represent it in an organizational chart. Draw the chart as it should be at the end of the third year of business. Use dotted lines for the fill-these-positions-later boxes, and use solid lines for the boxes to contain the positions to be filled from the start. Is all of this hard work worth the effort? Definitely, it is. Here is what you will be accomplishing: 1) you are forcing yourself into a realistic appraisal of the problems associated with growth, and 2) prospective investors will see that you are fully aware of the fact that you cannot always do everything yourself.

When I look at a potential investment, one of my main requirements is that the business plan must show how the business will continue to grow if and when the founder leaves.

Refer to this organizational chart at frequent intervals as your business develops, and especially whenever you need to make decisions that will affect the lives and performances of those working for you. That vice president for whom you are looking may have been working for you for the last two years!

There is always some fear involved in the turning loose of the reins of authority, but, more often than not, you will be amply rewarded for having faith in your employees. In small, growing concerns, wages and other benefits are often well below those of larger companies in your industry. Your employees, however, are often of a much higher caliber than industry standard. Why is this? It is because the better people work both for money and for things more important than money. They work for the satisfaction of helping to build something new and for recognition of their own importance. Not everyone can get big prizes like the Nobel, a Pulitzer, or an Oscar - but everyone can win the prize of being recognized for a job well done. Call this prize the Entrepreneur Prize. You are the one who awards it. If you will remember that, you will be able to build a team that can overcome the obstacles that will appear in front of your business as it moves down the pathway to prosperity.

As you construct your organizational chart, develop introductory remarks that explain how the unfilled positions will be handled as the business grows. Try to show the timing of adding new people to the staff. Be sure to review the departmental budgets to insure that you have correctly allocated the funds these new salaries will require.

In all of your business dealings you will discover that you will have more pain, more trouble, and much more joy in dealing with the people around you than with any other aspect of being an entrepreneur. No matter how great a dreamer you are, and no matter how great a business you build, none of it will ever become reality without people. If you do your job well in selecting and managing people you may be fortunate enough to find that there is another entrepreneur on your staff. If so, encourage him or her. Don't hold that person back. Place responsibility on this individual and let it be known that you are offering both respect and trust. Your reward for this investment may not always be monetary, but helping others to expand their own horizons will bring you the most long lasting rewards.

If you gain a reputation for being fair and for sharing responsibility and authority, the good people will find you.

Conversely, as Malcolm Forbes once said, "If you want to be the whole deal no one will want to deal with you... other than to deal you out ."

Becoming an entrepreneur doesn't mean being the whole deal. It means being smart enough to build a team that can do things together that you could never accomplish by yourself.

Section 6 - Internal Operations

Not all business plans need a section covering internal operations. I have included this section in the discussion so as to encourage entrepreneurs to give considerable thought to the operating structures of their staff right from the start.

Larger businesses use this section of their plans to focus on particular aspects of their businesses, such as customer service, repair service, inventory control, and so on. A new or small business can use this section to demonstrate the fact that operating questions or problems that come to mind with readings of previous sections of the plan have all been considered. Here is where you show the steps that are being taken to deal with these situations. In order to better decide what needs to be included in this section, it is necessary to first consider the scope of the internal operations of your business.

The story is told of a man who was elected president of a large company. One of the older directors, while congratulating the man, smiled and said, "Congratulations, you have heard the truth for the last time."

While the story is quite cynical, I believe that it makes a valid point. A sound organizational structure should provide all of the information needed for decision making to those people charged with making the decisions. To prevent yourself from becoming isolated in your own company, pay attention to the way information flow is organized. If you are not getting the proper information, you may be in for a shock or two if, later, reality is suddenly thrust upon you.

The key to successful organization is simplicity. When you are doing everything yourself, everything about your organization is simple. The idea, then, is to keep the simplicity as you grow.

Again, let's use the example of that newsletter company, Charter Boating Newsletters, to illustrate how to work up the manpower section of your business plan.

Assume that a subscription for the newsletter came by mail today, along with a check in payment. What has to be done? Well, the check needs to be endorsed and deposited in the bank account, the subscriber's name has to be entered on the subscription list, the name and date must be placed on the tickler list for contacting at renewal time, a letter of thanks is to be sent to the new subscriber, and there are probably several other things that need to be done right away. With growth in mind the newsletter owner has written out a simple, one page explanation of each step to be accomplished in handling this incoming subscription. Keep each separable task on a single sheet of paper (for one day you might need to have a whole department just to open the mail and separate the checks from the orders!)

When the order came in, did you mark the order "paid" and did you enter the check number on the order? Write the steps down as you actually do them.

One entrepreneur I know not only wrote out each task as he accomplished it, he actually moved from desk to desk in his new office. When there were finally other people doing the jobs, he could walk through the office and judge the status of the day's business simply by observing what was happening at each desk. Another advantage he gained by assigning each task a different physical location (even in light of the fact that there were only two employees and seven work stations...) was that he could immediately spot any potential bottleneck that might reduce the efficiency of his order processing department.

When working out internal operations, pay close attention to each and every detail, even the minute ones. A good entrepreneur is aware of even the smallest detail. Sure, the entrepreneur is supposed to be an idea person, but I have learned to never really trust a proponent of a business plan who would not be bothered with details. Don't get buried under details, but be aware of their importance - and take time to listen to your employees' suggestions and criticisms of existing operations. Often, small details are the ones that can make or break a new business.

As soon as some of the initial organizational activities are written down, concentrate on the key activities and discuss these in your business plan - describing how you intend to streamline them and still maintain a good grasp on what is going on daily in your business. Here is another word of caution. Be careful to set up your internal operations in a way that allows the daily operation of your business to progress smoothly without your direct intervention. All too often a company's operating procedures resemble the shape of a soda pop bottle, the bottleneck being at the top. If you insist on having a hand in everything going on, you will strangle your business.

Part Four - Money How To Get It - How To Keep It

Don't Let The Excuses Fly For You

January 16th.

It is hard to believe that I completed four hours of in-flight instruction during the first nine days of training, but, during the past four months I have flown only another four hours. When I began ballooning I was so sure that I would have my license by October and, yet, I still have a long way to go. There are many reasons (excuses), of course: bad weather, business matters, lack of a ground crew, and on and on. But the fact remains that if I had really set my mind to it I could have had my license by now.

Maybe I need to re-examine my desire to fly. Maybe it is nothing more than a passing fancy. However, if I don't see this balloon license project through to completion I will have taken a major step backward. Yes! I will see this project through to a conclusion. After I am licensed I can decide whether or not I care to continue flying.

Money

"You don't have a money problem. You just have an idea

problem."
Dr. Robert Schuler

So, here you are. You have a great idea. You have developed your idea into a well organized business plan, and now you can't get the business started because it will take more money than you can see from where you stand. You might as well give up, right?

Maybe this has happened to you before. This time, however, you have really thought your plan through, organized it on paper and, perhaps, even tested out some of it to see how viable it is. All you need now is a little money or, perhaps, a lot of money. No problem!

As much as I dislike the thought, money is fuel. Money is power. Without fuel you can't run the engines. Without power you cannot advance your cause and, at the same time, protect it from attack from the rear and sides. Without money you cannot really improve your own lot nor the lots of others. Money, itself, is not that all-fired important. It is the lack of money that is important. You don't have enough money on hand to start your new business? From where, then, is it to come?

Many people who start their first business obtain the required capital from friends, neighbors, and relatives. The emphasis is on the words, "first business." Once you have been in business, whether or not the business was successful, you will find it easier to raise money for another business. Friends, neighbors, and relatives are difficult lenders with whom to contend. There will be much unwanted advice, emotional strains, and other discomforts.

If the funds are available from friends, neighbors, and relatives - but from nowhere else - you have but one choice to make.

However, there are other sources of start-up capital that are at times available. Before you run out to take advantage of them, you should get organized for the task. Let's take a look at the five points a business person must consider when seeking money:

1. Your cash requirements both for the short term and the long term

2. The method you will use to raise that cash

3. The handling of the money when it comes in

4. The profit potential that has to be there to cause the cash to grow

5. How to retain some of this profit for yourself

The last three points, above, are vital points. If you cannot satisfy them adequately, you may later wish you had never started your business - or you may not even be able to start it. It is going to be up to you to satisfy these guidelines, but this part of the book will help provide you with a framework for doing that.

Determining cash requirements

"The use of money is all the advantage there is in having money."
Benjamin Franklin

Many businesses have their beginning something like this:

1) a discussion in a coffee shop;

2) some figures written on a napkin; and

3) a checking account as the only financial record for the first six months!

My first business (like so many others begun with as little preparation) actually prospered for the first two years. However, with growth, the problems began to surface. I asked myself how I might have predicted the problems early enough to prevent them or solve them before they became insurmountable.

Some folks, particularly accountants, maintain that anyone who does not understand cash flow should stay out of business. That may or may not be the case, but it is possible for the non-accountant to safely and securely predict cash flow and cash requirements.

Here is a simplified way to look at cash flow by listing your requirements as follows:

> Beginning cash
> Cash in
> Loans
> Other cash in
> Total cash in
> Cash out – operations
> Cash out – Inventory
> Loan repayments
> Total cash out
> Ending cash

These items are rather self-explanatory. Now I will show you the procedure I use to determine some of the numbers .

Starting with the first month of the business plan, the beginning cash amount is easy to determine. It is the amount of cash you have on hand to put into the business. Next comes CASH IN. This amount is the same as net sales for cash and carry businesses, but, for most businesses you will have to account for credit purchases and delayed payments. So assume that the sales will be made and that the cash will come in according to some delayed, but reasonably predictable, pattern. Overestimate the credit still out there and underestimate the cash payments - it is safer. Now, skip ahead and enter the figure for CASH OUT - OPERATIONS. This number should be the same as the one shown for your total expenses (sum of the departmental budgets).

CASH OUT - INVENTORY is more complicated. The key to determining how much money you must have each month to maintain the inventory will be based on the length of time it takes to receive goods ordered, the volume of goods needed in the inventory at all times, the reduction of inventory by sales each month, and, of course, the cost per unit of the inventory.

Once you have determined the above cash in and cash out requirements for every month of your business plan, you are in a position to complete the remaining items on the cash flow section of your pro-forma financial statement. Subtract TOTAL CASH OUT from TOTAL CASH IN. The sum shown will be the amount of extra cash you will need to have available from month to month. In most instances, this extra cash need will rise for a number of months and will then decline. If that is so, you have planned well - sooner or later you will break into the profit picture and be able to pay back some cash shortages encountered in the beginning. The maximum amount of these cash shortages is, therefore, the amount of capital you need to fund your business.

The questions then become:

Do you obtain that cash as a loan?

Do you obtain that cash as investment capital?

Do you obtain that cash all at once?

Do you obtain that cash as you need it?

Do you combine these techniques?

Your answers will vary depending upon the nature of your business - and how much money you have to invest yourself. Some businesses continue to grow very rapidly and constantly need additional cash. If that is to be the nature of your business, you must establish a line of credit at the beginning. For other businesses, the entrepreneur may be able to fund the entire amount of start-up capital without any additional loans or investors. If loans are involved, you will have to set up the means to repay those loans - and the repayments will have to be included in all cash flow statements. It all comes down to your having to balance your cash needs with either income, credit, loans, or additional investment capital. To make it even simpler, it is the same as having to watch your budget at home and having to match your income and spending.

With an understanding of cash requirements you will be well prepared to discuss raising the capital you need to start things rolling. Be conversant with cash flow and all it encompasses, for that will put you in a strong position to plead your case to any necessary investors.

Raising the initial capital

"One of life's disappointments is discovering that the person who writes advertising copy for a bank is not the person who approves requests for loans."
Anonymous

Most funds for new, small businesses come from friends, neighbors, and relatives of the entrepreneurs. I know of situations where close friends or relatives offered to *give* money to new entrepreneurs. Talk about potential trouble.

Back in my starting-up days I had the unpleasant experience of trying for weeks to get an appointment with a venture capitalist only to finally walk in with my three page proposal and an ill-prepared presentation. I should have been laughed out of the room - but I wasn't. I learned something that day. In fact, the experience had a lot to do with my writing this book. By your preparing a well thought out, detailed business plan, you have taken a giant step. Put yourself in an investor's place. Wouldn't you look more favorably upon a well-prepared plan more than you would upon a few loose sheets of paper on which a possibly good idea might be described? That well thought out, detailed business plan should include everything thus far described in this book.

So how do you get ready to make your presentations to those from whom you would seek capital investment? One recommendation is to practice your presentation on your friends, neighbors, and relatives. They can be excellent critics. You should hope that they ask you difficult to answer questions. In that way, and in other ways, those close to you may help you locate areas in your plan needing revision.

It sometimes happens that a friend or relative who is helping you with one of these practice sessions gets excited to the point of asking you if they might invest in your new company. If that happens, be considerate but be careful. Don't flatly reject them. Tell them that you are in the process of discussing investments with several venture capital sources and that you feel it important to follow through with those talks. Mention, that when you get all the facts assembled, you will get back to them so as to possibly work something out. Don't burn any bridges! If you get the capital you need from the venture capitalists, do get back to your friends and relatives and explain to them that your deals went through all right. If you get no outside capital that way, get back to your friends and relatives and tell them that you are ready to listen to what they have to say - and to offer!

Loan providers or equity partners? Which should it be? Both have pros and both have cons. If you can get a loan of sufficient size you will retain control over your business - but you will receive very little outside direction and counseling, A venture capitalist, on the other hand, will be co-owner with you - but will also act as a powerful source of guidance that can really help you to succeed. If you decide on the latter course, the equity partnership with a venture capital provider, you have to understand how much of your company it is that you are willing to relinquish. Most venture capital organizations and individuals prefer to hold a 55% (or more) interest in an entrepreneur's first project.

You may believe that 55% interest demanded by the venture capitalists is unfair. After all, wasn't the whole idea yours? Who is it who will be working twenty hours a day for the next few years to insure success? Why should someone who simply put up some seed money take the majority of your company? Think of it this way: If you had been doing the things being done by your venture capitalist over the last several years, you might have piled up a couple of million dollars or more to be re-invested in other new ventures. If that were your money, wouldn't you be careful where you put it? Venture capitalists are not ten-per-cent sorts of people. They like to win big. Consequently, they frequently lose big. They lose ALL of their investment in at least half of the situations - and that is why they are forced to want to control your business during the time it is at its highest risk - at the start.

Before approaching a venture capital source you should find out all you can about the individuals and groups comprising the industry. Venture capitalists specialize. Some invest only in high-tech industries. Others concentrate in retailing, manufacturing, and other sorts of industries. Try to find out how many successful start ups each venture capital group has funded. Some groups wait until a venture is a year or two (or more) old before they will consider it as an investment. Other groups prefer to fund pure start ups. Try to sort out the venture capital groups that might have an interest in your company from the ones who truly wouldn't give your company a second glance. Then, when you are ready, contact the presidents of those companies funded by the venture capital groups in which you have an interest. Ask each how they feel about their backers. Seldom will a company president pull any punches when discussing venture capitalists. You will either be told that their experience with their venture capitalists has been great - or you will be warned to stay away from them!

Your public library can be a good source of reference books about venture capital and venture capitalists. Those reference books include texts on the general subject of venture capital and listings of venture capital funds. Before you make up your mind - loan or sale of equity interest - do your research.

But what if you have had practice capital-seeking sessions with friends, relatives, and neighbors, and then, after that, you visited every venture capitalist within travel distance. You then mailed your business plan to every source of venture capital you located. After that, you solicited funding from every bank in your area. Then you approached various sources of government funding... but you have yet to come up with the necessary capital to get your new business going. What can you do now? Quit? Change your idea? Well, you could do those things, but there is another avenue open to you for travel: **You can start your business without any seed money other than your own!** That's right. You can simply start your business in motion with no outside capital - no loans - not even a how-do-you-do! How can this be done? If the funds are not available elsewhere, "poor boy" it. Here's how.

Examine your business plan carefully. Make a listing of all of the tasks that need doing and that require time and effort rather than money. Now, get to work on those tasks and don't worry that all of your hard work might be in vain in the event you don't find a source of venture capital. Just get started. You will be amazed at what can happen. Let me give you an example.

A friend of mine worked as a salesman for a real estate company. I will call him Clyde Comfortable here. Clyde's passion was personal computers - in fact, he built one for himself. He read everything that came out about the new models and about the new programs. Clyde wanted to get out of the real estate business and into the computer business. Unfortunately, Clyde's current salary was high - unfortunately because Clyde was making enough money to keep him and his family very comfortable. Comfortable people rarely quit their present jobs and start over again. Clyde couldn't push computers from his mind, however, so he constructed a business plan calling for the establishment of a group of knowledgeable consultants who would call on businesses to help them select small computer systems to fit their needs. As excellent an approach as that one seemed, it caused Clyde to be turned down by potential investors. The plan didn't call for actually selling computers - it envisioned only receipt of a percentage of the purchase price spent by the client for equipment. The investors told Clyde that they would probably back him if he would represent and sell one or two lines of computers. Clyde stood firm. He didn't want to have a computer store as his business.

Well, Clyde didn't have enough money to open his office, hire a secretary, or build a staff of consultants. So Clyde began to do the things that cost little or no out-of-pocket money. He contacted owners of small businesses by telephone, telling each that he would send a letter explaining his services. Several days after mailing the letters, he called back to see if the business owners had questions. From that slow and tedious beginning, Clyde eventually picked up two clients. He didn't earn much money from either of them, but his computer business was started. It was HIS! In about two years he had built up his part-time business to the point where people were asking him if he were interested in expanding - and, if so, would he allow them to invest in his company. Clyde's beginning in business was not spectacular, but he now owns a thriving company! The key was that Clyde actually got started. Maybe the way he had to start was not the way he had it all planned, but a little momentum is a wondrous thing. Put some motion behind your business ideas and watch them soar from a small start to surprising heights!

The search for initial capital can be frustrating and complicated. It really shouldn't be that way. You will hear many "no's," but it takes only one or two "yes's" to get you on your way. You have to ask for initial capital in order to get your yes and no answers. The solution may be as simple as your receiving lots of "no's" so that you will finally ask that venture capitalist who will tell you, "Yes!" Too often we search for complicated answers to simple problems. If you ask enough people, someone will eventually agree to back you.

It is of interest that your present employer, if you are a great employee, may decide to back you in a new venture. Many employers really want to help and they will do whatever it takes, including putting up the initial money for a new business. There is a story told about a close friend of Henry Ford. He sold insurance, and one morning he read in the newspaper that Ford had just purchased a huge insurance policy from another agent. He placed a telephone call to Henry Ford and asked, "Why didn't you buy your insurance from me?" Ford replied, "You never asked me!"

One final thought. As you search for money, don't let the facts get in the way of your emotions. A strong, factual presentation is important, but investors don't base decisions on the facts nearly as often as they base them on emotions. Obviously, you feel very strongly about your new business. You need to convey those feelings to the investors. You might win them over more quickly by enlisting their feelings than you can by convincing their reasoning.

Money - How To Handle It

"I'm not saying that chance doesn't sometimes open the door. But luck belongs to the good players ."
Bernard Baruch

Let's assume that you have raised the start up capital required for the first year of operation. Now that you have the problem of finding start up money out of the way, you may think that all of your problems are over. Wrong! You have cleared a major hurdle, but often *handling* money is sometimes harder to do than finding it. Your salvation may

135

turn out to be that carefully prepared business plan. You can win the battle of money management by matching the monthly expenditures with the proposed budgets.

Amazingly, many otherwise intelligent people spend days and weeks working out budgets and pro-forma cash flow statements. Then they put them aside after beginning their business operations. You should use your budget to help you control your monthly cash-out. If your business is headed for trouble, the early warning signal will appear as you compare your pro-forma and the results of the month's operations.

You should try to spend a little under budget each, month, for your sales may be less than projected. Whenever you or a staff member are about to order some necessity, make it a rule that you will first try to find a way to do without the thing. Use your buying dollars to buy things that will contribute most directly to your profitability.

There is often a danger to a new business that, as soon as money begins to flow freely, financial controls are relaxed. Don't give in to such a temptation. When you relax your money controls, you give away production and profit. Respect the money that comes into your business. Money is both a terrible master and an excellent servant. **Don't waste a penny!** Try to come up with a way to remember that advice every day of your business life. Always look for creative ways to save your money and to put it to work.

Here is an example of that creativity at work. An entrepreneur had just printed three million copies of Theodore Roosevelt's 1912 convention speech. He was ready to ship the prints to customers when he woke up to the fact that he had failed to obtain permission from the photographer whose pictures were used in the reprints. Rather than throw it all away, he sent the photographer this telegram:

"Planning to issue 3 million copies of Roosevelt speech with pictures on cover. Great publicity opportunity for photographers. What will you pay us to use your photographs?"

An hour later he received this reply: "Appreciate opportunity, but can pay only $250."

Keep that example in mind whenever you get ready to throw away some money!

Bob Edwards said that making money first is not what is important - it is making money last! That is pretty good advice. You will discover that making money last is important - and that it is a time consuming task. I'm not saying that you should never turn the financial controls of your business over to someone else, but it is my opinion that the owner should always approve all major expenditures of the company's money. As the business grows, this control will take the form of monitoring departmental budgets, but, in the beginning, it means signing every check. The quickest way to lose control of your business is to give up the control of its checkbook.

Organisms seem to have a universal desire to live beyond their means. It is the same for businesses. The desire may always be present, but you need not give in to it. So, when you spend some hard earned cash, make sure that you spend it on things that will enhance your ability to bring in larger profits. If you spend all of your start up capital before the business is properly functioning, its survival is far less likely. The initial funding is to insure survival, so that, when you spend it with no replacement in sight, survival goes out the window with the cash! There is another thing to consider. If you develop a constant cash shortage, you will find that most of your time will be spent in trying to overcome that problem. Your productive time should be spent thinking of how to hit the market with your products and services - how to improve your business - not in dealing with angry creditors and unhappy customers. If you let your business get into that fix, you are on quicksand, and the chances of survival are slim.

Sitting at your desk instead of getting on out there to advance your business interests is one sign of being constantly under financial attack - having to deal with financial crises. Entrepreneurs should beware of the temptation to sit in the office, letting people come to them. Hurry about, talk to customers, solve problems, and keep people excited about the prospects of the business. Sitting behind a desk all the time causes the business to stagnate. If all you want is a job, you can safely get into some sort of routine - sitting behind a desk is one of them. As an entrepreneur you will quickly discover that it is not comfort that brings satisfaction - it is hard work and lots of action.

Your business plan is the rock on which you can lean when, as your business continues to grow it begins to have a momentum all its own. Once the money begins to generate itself, so to speak, you had better be prepared to ride with it or to get out of the business altogether. You can be carried to dizzying heights and you can be dropped to the ground so quickly that you may never know what happened to you. Don't panic. You have your business plan. You can always tell where you are in relation to the plan. When you know who you are and where you are, you can deal with whatever may come your way.

Money - Is There Really A Profit?

"Life is a misery if you don't get more than you deserve."
Harry Oppenheimer

Profit may be a dirty word to many people, but if you really want a dirty word, try this one: "loss." You see, even so-called non-profit enterprises still have to bring in more money than they pay out if they want to remain alive. Profits are the life-blood of a business. They are not bad in and of themselves. What greedy people do with their excess earnings, however, is what gives the word "profit" a bad name.

My dictionary defines profit as: "Compensation accruing to entrepreneurs for the assumption of risk in business enterprises."

Is there really something wrong with paying people to assume risk? During my lifetime I have had to deal with my share of people who seem to think it immoral to make a profit. Without profit there can be no funds available for future growth and expansion.

Earning profits does not mean cheating customers, suppliers, employees, or backers. Especially, it does not mean taking advantage of your employees. You will discover that if you pay a person less than he or she is worth, he or she will soon be worth less than he or she is paid. Likewise, you must be fair with your customers. It is, in the end, only their goodwill that will keep you in business. You cannot buy goodwill for any amount of money. Like profit, it must be earned.

Any transaction by which one person gains and another loses is, quite simply, a fraud. A good deal is one in which both parties gain. There is no need to rob people in order to make a profit. Be honest. Give your customers a fair price. Be sure you give value for the money and don't encourage poor people to spend needlessly.

Be sure your business is designed to make good profits. You may have the greatest idea in all the world, but if it won't generate profits you had best begin looking for another idea. Entrepreneurs deal with profitable ideas and reject those that are losers. If what you propose to do (or are doing) is useful, then your business will return good profits to you. There is an old Hindu proverb that declares: "Help thy brother's boat across, and, lo, thine own has reached the shore."

Look for ways to improve some quality of life for other people and you will more than likely come upon a profitable idea.

Part Four Summary

1. Prepare a detailed cash flow analysis of your business

2. Begin talking to money sources

3. Match each month's cash-out with the budget to pick up early warning signs of trouble

4. Don't begin until you are sure you can make solid profits

Part Five – Enterprise Killers

Jack Cannot – Balloon Hater!

March 3rd.

I'm afraid of tomorrow. Compared to driving on the freeway, a high velocity descent from five thousand feet may be a tranquil experience, but it is an experience with which I am as yet unfamiliar. My instructor has explained that our balloon will spiral downward at the rate of about fifteen hundred feet a minute, and that caution must be exercised to recover flight stability gradually. My instructor has been through this maneuver many times. He will be with me. Why then do I lie awake and worry?

March 4th,

I did it! In fact, it wasn't really that much of an event. Instead of worrying about crashing, I should have been worrying about the reception committee we would encounter on the ground. Upon landing, we were met by an irate tenant farmer, Jack Cannot. Although we had not damaged anything with our balloon, landing in an unplanted field as we did, Jack Cannot called the sheriff and asked him to arrest us for trespassing. The sheriff knew the law, understood that balloons cannot stay up forever, and he also knew Jack Cannot. He let us take our balloon and leave. Later, we found out that Jack Cannot was an unhappy tenant farmer who couldn't stand to see others enjoying life. I now wonder if the thrill of flight is worth the

143

hassle of dealing with such counter-productive people - like Jack Cannot.

Running The Gauntlet

"Why... some of my best friends are farmers!"
King George III

The question may be how to deal with so many people who don't think just like we do. The entrepreneur, just like the balloon pilot, must spend more time on the ground than in the air. And it is on the ground that you will encounter the most difficulties. While you are flying up there with your dreams, the world below will be distant enough to look beautiful - it is only when you are back down on the muddy earth, face to face with some tenant farmer of life, that you, too, might question the worth of the struggle.

Please don't think that I have anything against tenant farmers. My grandfather was one, and he was a magnificent person. When I speak of the tenant farmers of life I am talking about those people who only use things, never adding value, never contributing ideas. Who are these people?

As an entrepreneur, you must learn the lessons of the pilot. You are totally alone in your adventure. It is you and only you on whom you must depend. Ask for help. Ask for advice. But in the end you must be like the captain who trusts only his ship and himself. The fact that you cannot put much faith in others may seem to be a terrible thing, but it is a law of survival. In this part of the book I hope to give you a few other ideas about how to utilize this law and yet remain a warm and loving human being in the process. It is quite a trick, but the great entrepreneurs have all managed to perform it.

Traveling through a gauntlet of enterprise killers, you will be surprised at who some of them are. Some are close friends. Some are relatives and neighbors. At times you may notice that they are among your competitors. Often they will be accountants and lawyers. Very often they are non-producers, such as bureaucrats or civil (or uncivil) servants as they may be called.

Let's take a look at the various things that can happen to you – and let's look at the gremlins out there waiting to pounce on your plans. Then we shall examine what can be done about them.

Dealing With Friends

"When a true genius appears in the world, you may know him by this sign, that the dunces are all in confederacy against him."
Jonathan Swift

It seems such a shame that those who know us best and care most about us are usually the ones who will be hardest to convince that we are doing the right thing. For years, I spent a lot of time trying to figure this out. So far, I haven't come up with a satisfactory answer. In talking with other people who have experienced the rejection of their ideas by those closest to them, I find that more often than not people seem to instinctively feel that if the new idea is a resounding success their relationship to the entrepreneur will change. Actually, this fear is reasonably grounded. For, successful or not, the entrepreneur will experience great personal growth. If his or her associates don't also find a way to grow, they will be left behind. Perhaps it is this fear of being left behind that pushes friends, relatives, and neighbors to downgrade an entrepreneur's dreams.

Learning how to deal with these enterprise killers has been one of the most difficult things I have had to learn along the way. I have found that there are no set guidelines that can be followed, since both entrepreneur and enterprise are constantly growing - and the situation is in constant flux. Along the way you will meet different types of resistance. If the business is having difficulty, people will react differently than they will when you first present your ideas. It may come as a shock that if your business fails you will often have more support from those closest to you than you will if it succeeds. This world of ours is strange, isn't it?

To avoid criticism you need only do nothing, say nothing, and be nothing. Entrepreneurs cannot avoid criticism. You must learn to live with it. Think of yourself as the builder of a business - much like the builder of a barn. Any jackass can kick down the wall of a barn, but it takes a good builder to make that wall. When people criticize you, think of that.

Why do people reject the grand ideas of their closest associates? Have you ever put down someone's new idea without first thinking it through? Of course you have. Ideas, being abstract visualizations, can be hard to explain and difficult to grasp. Add to that the fact that we tend to label people - they may be labeled as gullible, calculating, shrewd, dull, highly intelligent, a pretty face, a real jerk! It is easier to pass judgment on the person than on his or her idea.

Also, you must watch out for bad advice. Remember, age alone does not mean wisdom. Assess the significance of the adviser's experience - not the age. Often enough, the person being asked for advice has had much experience - and all of it the same! All too often such people are no longer young enough to set bad examples - so they give bad advice instead.

One reason causing a person to discuss a new business plan with close friends is for affirmation that they are on the right track. If you have this motive, take care to present your ideas in completely honest ways. The comments you receive will have a strong impact on what you do next. You should seek positive responses, but you should pay attention if the responses are mostly negative. You want serious criticism. If you get some negative remarks, say "thank you" and then give some serious thought to what you were told. Be completely honest with your critics and with yourself. Don't lie to yourself just to keep going. If you lie to yourself, you will soon be lying to others. Your lack of forthrightness will hurt you a whole lot more than it will hurt those from whom you withheld the truth.

So, don't go to your friends, relatives, and neighbors for a pat on the back, telling wild stories about how successful your new business is. Avoid putting your business in front of them unless they can truly help you by providing advice, money, or time. At all costs, avoid arguing with your close associates. Listen to all well-intended criticism, and don't get angry with people who tell you what to them is the truth. You can adjust your plans to account for problems your associates may point out, but don't let a critic sway you from your path. And furthermore, don't discontinue an association simply because someone isn't as excited about your idea as you are. From their points of view, your friends, relatives, and neighbors are only doing and saying what they think is best for you. They honestly care about you. Just because they don't see the same vision you see doesn't mean that they aren't on your side. Explain, listen, and then keep your own counsel.

The Bureaucratic Jungle

"Families, when a child is born, want it to be intelligent. I, through intelligence, having wrecked my whole life, only hope the baby will prove ignorant and stupid. Then he will crown a tranquil life by becoming a cabinet minister."
Su Tung-p'o *(A.D. 1036-1101)*

Had Su Trung-p'o lived to see the twentieth century he would not have been very surprised to note that functionaries remained as before. Who are these people, and why do we allow some of them to control so much of our lives?

While it might be possible to write thousands of pages on this topic, I had best simply provide you with a few guidelines for dealing with what may be the main problem faced by every person engaged in business - the problem of dealing with a seemingly endless series of bureaucratic regulations, procedures, and uninterested clerks.

Pretend for a moment that government clerks are the same as pieces of office equipment. When your copying machine breaks down, you can yell and scream, and even hit it, yet the machine will still do nothing. Government clerks are a lot like broken copying machines. They don't respond to yelling and screaming, and they definitely don't deserve violence. When you deal with clerks and legislators – bureaucrats and government functionaries – keep in mind that you are not dealing with highly motivated people.

This brings us to a second rule. Deal with a bureaucrat as you would deal with a child. Don't stoop to their level. Try to bring them up to your level. Follow that rule and your life can be easier. Clerks and legislators, like the branches of government they represent, have only as much control over you as you allow them to have. All you want to do is to run your business, create new jobs, earn a profit, and add to the nation's economy. So how do you deal with these sometimes petty tyrants - the clerks and legislators? Be firm. Be fair. Understand who they are and why they are there, and don't resent them personally.

Remember, you have nothing about which to feel guilty. You are about to do one of the noblest things a person can do - create a new business to feed, clothe, shelter, and employ others who don't yet have your amount of skill and courage. You are an entrepreneur, and dealing with government regulations and those who enforce them just goes with the territory.

149

Professional Enterprise Killers

"Lawyers are like beavers... they get in the mainstream and dam it up."
John Naisbitt

Professionals. Isn't it comforting that there are so many highly specialized people whose opinions you can elicit as you build your new business? Comforting, yes. Helpful, no. This may be the first book you have ever read that advises against obtaining professional opinions when first forming a new business plan. If there is a collection of people deserving to be listed under the heading of enterprise killers it consists of lawyers, accountants, and bankers - professionals. Yes, you will find them all to be useful, even necessary, at times, but in the early days of your business they only serve to dam things up.

First, let's take up the subject of bankers. Bankers should be used to provide you with the easy means to handle your money. They are good for checking accounts and fund transfers. If you need advice, however, it is best to avoid bankers. If bankers were good at giving investment advice, they would have better records in their handling of pension funds and other trust accounts. Further, you can forget about bankers as sources of start up capital. Dismiss the thought of bankers for any type of true business loans for the first five or ten years of your business. Bankers do make loans, but loans to the younger businesses are typically secured by assets worth at least twice the amount of the loan - and, more typically, they merely loan you your own money.

In addition to being unable or unwilling to do anything positive to help you, your friendly banker can, and often will, bury you. Banks are businesses. In recent years banks have been performing poorly. The papers have been full of news of bank failures - some of them really big crashes! When a bank gets into a cash bind, you can bet that the first people to feel the pinch will be the bank's small business customers. In many instances a bank's internal problems will have bad effects on very large, but very young, companies. The cancellation of a previously approved line of credit to Osborne Computer Company forced that spectacularly successful corporation into Chapter 11 bankruptcy after Osborne had achieved sales of $100 million during its second year in business. How's that for a friendly banker? What is the bottom line on bankers? Forget them. They will never be of any great help to the entrepreneur.

What about accountants? If you think of them in the same way you think of auto mechanics you will be all right. You should tell your accountant what it is you want done, and it is his or her job to assemble the information you need and to complete the paperwork satisfactorily.

Accountants should make reports to you about how and where your money went or is heading. Your accountant should prepare your company tax reports and the internal reports you will use in your own planning and for the information of your investors. Beyond that you should not ask for much help from accountants. Their problem, if indeed it is a problem, is that accountants are not risk takers. They look on any new venture as being too risky. If you seek the advice of an accountant too early in your business, you will come away wondering why it was you even thought of starting your company. What is the bottom line on accountants? They are certainly more helpful than bankers, but should be used as one would use mechanics.

Now we come to those really deadly enterprise killers (second only to government functionaries in bad effects...) - the lawyers. Years ago, when I was still a law student, I resented Shakespeare' famous line, "First we must kill all the lawyers."

After four years as a practicing attorney, however, I came to understand why he wrote that. Lawyers are trained to see only the negative aspects of things. It is a rare attorney who looks for reasons why a project will work. The majority of them concentrate on finding flaws in everything.

Once I was representing a land title insurance company at a very large real estate closing. All of the parties met at nine in the morning for what was supposed to be a simple signing of documents. Both parties showed up with their attorneys - and then the fun began. One attorney would point out some area that, one day, might cause a problem. Then the attorney for the other party would do the same sort of thing so that he, too, could justify a large fee. This process went on and on. The lawyers argued far into the night such that the meeting had to be continued the next day. I was there only to issue a title insurance policy, and so I had the opportunity to watch this process as an outsider. It was then that I first became aware of how easy it is for lawyers to kill good business deals. Most lawyers feel that if they don't point out every single flaw in a project they are being negligent. Yet, a person in business already knows the risks involved, so that all an attorney should do is write the contract as well as can be done so as not to add any extra risks.

There was an interesting ending to this marathon property closing session. As the parties were just about to call the whole deal off, an outside attorney was brought in to mediate between the parties. Fortunately, this lawyer was one who understood his function in the world. Instead of reading the piles of documents on the table before giving an opinion, he simply asked two questions: "Do you, seller, want to sell this property? Do you, buyer, want to buy this property?"

There were two "yes" replies, after which this high-powered lawyer remarked that it looked as though the parties had done the deal - and that all that remained to be accomplished was the ironing out of a few details. An hour later all of the papers had been signed and everyone was smiling.

You can see what a difference an attorney with a positive attitude can make. Now, try to find an attorney like that. Believe me, they are few and far between. For some reason the practice of law seems to promote negative attitudes in the people who practice it. As attorneys gain success and money, their reputations grow. Before long they tend to believe their own press, thinking themselves now to be omnipotent sources of all business wisdom. But, before taking business advice from an attorney, ask what the attorney's pre-tax net income was as a percent of his billable income. If the law business is not all that profitable, can the lawyer be a good source of advice to you regarding your business? Despite all this, some people still think that lawyers know all the answers.

Lawyers tend to answer all questions with such force and conviction that people feel that their answers must be correct. Actually that is the dogma and style the lawyers pick up as they learn their trade. The greater the ignorance, the greater the dogmatism. Many attorneys become so fixed in their thinking that they stop thinking altogether. There will be times when you will need the advice of an attorney, but you surely don't need their advice as to whether or not you should be in business. I use my attorney this way - I tell him what I am going to do, and then I ask him to help me be certain that nothing I am about to do will violate any laws. I couldn't care less if he thinks that I am about to launch a failure. Remember, though, attorneys tend to think of themselves as authorities on everything, so stand by for some unwanted advice!

Here is a final word of caution about attorneys. No matter how much money you think it may save you, don't ever let an attorney take an interest in your company in exchange for legal services. Most reputable attorneys will never suggest such a thing, but there are too many lawyers who make this a common practice. There are thousands of entrepreneurs who lost everything once they took in attorneys as partners. When dining with wolves it makes little difference whether you are the guest or the main course.

Measuring The Competition

"A man comes to measure his greatness by the regrets, envies and hatreds of his competitors."
Emerson

Will your competitors help you measure your greatness by their envy - or will you measure their greatness by your envy of them? That's an interesting question. Let's begin a discussion about competition by stating the obvious - you will always have competition. Whenever I am shown a business plan that states there is no competition for that business, my first reaction is to throw the plan away. Be realistic. Even if you have created an entirely new product or service, it will not be long before others copy you. Accept competition and be glad. A good competitor will certainly help keep you on your toes. Competitors can be among your more valuable assets.

There are two different perspectives in which to view the competition: l) ahead of you; or 2) behind you. Be wary of thinking that you are solidly on top in a race with your competitors. You can't climb any higher if you already consider yourself to be at the top. If you reach the top of your mountain, it may be a good idea for you to look around and find a higher mountain in a big hurry.

Most business people that I know, however, constantly see themselves as underdogs. It is amusing to visit with the presidents of two competing companies and to learn from each of them that the other company is ahead. Things seem to look easy when the other guy is doing them. It is like watching a duck swim across a pond. The duck looks so calm and peaceful, and there is scarcely a ripple on the surface. The duck, however, is paddling like crazy below the water's surface. The same is true of your competition. It is no easier for them to stay even with you than it is for you to forge ahead of them. Many of your difficulties will be duplicated in their business. If you want to always be in the lead, you might best remember that you win more easily if you compete on your own terms – and on your own chosen ground.

Business is not really war, but there are a few similarities. Some of the root causes of war are the combination of desire for power, desire for territory, and desire for the ability to expand. Your objective in business is not to destroy your competition, but to conquer as much of their territory as you can while doing as little damage to it as possible. When competitors truly go to war, whole markets can be destroyed. An example of this is the battle in the early days of the personal computer industry between Texas Instruments, Atari, Commodore, and several other home computer manufacturing companies back in 1983 and 1984, which left a huge opening for IBM to come in and take over the entire market. The 'big three' of their day decided that total war was the only answer to competition, so they began cutting prices in attempts to drive the others out of that market. The more they cut prices, the more they lost on each sale. The result was that these companies either left the business or became second rate suppliers of cheap products. It took years for the home computer market to recover from that holocaust.

Even casual observers outside of that battle could see its inevitable conclusion. Yet, in the heat of battle, the generals refused to listen to reason. If you ever find yourself in such a situation, try to put yourself in your competitor's place. Why is he or she making those moves? On what are they basing their decisions? This is not as difficult to do as you might think. You need no spy inside the competitor's plant. Just read the trade journals, and you will have a pretty good idea of where your competition is.

Always play fair. If you don't play fair, it is as though you will have turned loose the wolf - and you will live to regret that. If you are in a position to put pressure on a competitor, try to leave them a way out. The great Chinese general Sun Tze always left his enemy an avenue of escape. A cornered adversary can be dangerous. You and your competitor, both, have the duty to survive. There is plenty of room for both of you. Don't try to kill each other. Just try to be the very best. Then there will be no doubt about the outcome.

Why did I put the competition in this section about enterprise killers? It is here as a reminder that the competition will not kill your business. Their effect on you is the effect you allow them to have. A tough competitor is a most valuable asset. If you don't simply lie down, your competitors cannot walk all over you. Stand upright and face them with enthusiasm. It is going to be a great game.

The King Of The Killers

"The only limits to our realization of tomorrow are our doubts of today."
Franklin D. Roosevelt

Failure. The fear of failure is an enterprise killer that can strike even before the business begins. Failure. What a frightening word. It sounds un-American, doesn't it? You have been exposed to numerous books, tapes, and seminars that expound on the ins and outs of failure, about the fact that one should believe that we will fail more often than we succeed. We have all heard of the baseball greats who strike out six times out of every ten tries. We know that the best of salespeople sell to fewer than one out of five prospects. You know that fear can and will paralyze you. Yet, you allow the fear of failure to creep into your thoughts every day. Why?

I cannot answer that question for you. I can only encourage you to spend some quiet time thinking up your own answer. What is it you fear? Why do you fear it? Once you answer those questions there will no longer be any need to be afraid. Overcome fear of failure and you will become one of those people blessed to lead fun-filled, exciting lives as opposed to those timid souls who make up the great mass of humanity. The time has come for you to break the bonds that hold you down. Break the chains of fear, frustration, and insecurity. Don't be afraid to fail. If there is no chance to fail, how can there be any chance to win?

Some people actually want to lose simply because they believe they do not deserve success. I saw this happen in the airport in Las Vegas. An elderly lady was playing the slot machines near the gate, and her friend was loudly urging her to quit. All of a sudden bells began ringing, and a crowd gathered around her to witness her success. She had put twenty-five cents into the machine and had just won five hundred dollars. There was much shouting and excitement - maybe even a few tears. It was good to see someone leave Las Vegas a winner. But then I heard the lady say to her companion that she couldn't believe she had won - and therefore she would give the companion one hundred dollars.

Why would this winner, who had risked her own money, want to give away part of her winnings to a friend who only moments before had been telling her that she ought to quit. I think she may have felt guilty about winning so much money with so little at risk. She felt guilty about winning! She really didn't think she deserved it. Well, entrepreneur, here is some good news for you. Every single dime you earn is very much deserved. In the past I have won big and I have lost big. The winnings and the losings were both well deserved. So forget about not deserving to win. If you have the courage to become an entrepreneur, you definitely deserve to win.

You have come this far. Don't let fear of failure *or* fear of winning stop you now. Open up a dozen businesses that fail if you must. You are an entrepreneur and have chosen to build a better world. Things won't happen exactly as you first envision them, and failure will no doubt come in one form or another, but don't fear. Success and failure have a common theme. Both show that you are trying. To try... to attempt... to go for it! That is what it is all about.

Consider this. Why would you want to attempt anything that had no risk of failure? Where is the glory in winning a victory that came without chance of loss? What do you actually stand to lose that is of real importance to you? Once you are able to isolate your sources of anxiety, you will be amazed at how quickly that anxiety turns into a stimulant. Make the tension work for you by seeing yourself climbing a sheer cliff. Yes, there is a chance that you may slip and fall. If you start to slip, you know that your heart will seem to stop. But, remember that you are still anchored to the mountain by your safety line. You may take a short fall, and when the safety line catches there will be a jolt that may take your breath away. Soon, however, you will catch your breath and, still alive, you will notice that you are much higher up the cliff than when you first began to climb. Now all you need do is to gain another toehold and begin climbing again.

What is this safety line that keeps you on the mountain? It is the understanding that, to an entrepreneur, success doesn't have anything to do with a single sale, or a single month's business, or even a single attempt at business. *To an entrepreneur, success is the progressive realization of a worthy ideal, never reaching the final goal, but constantly moving it higher and higher.*

One of my favorite movies is a documentary titled, "The Man Who Skied Down Everest." Just the thought of so awesome a feat makes my skin tingle. Think of it, skiing down the face of the world's highest mountain. It takes a person of unusual courage to even consider such an attempt, let alone carry it out. Yuichiro Miura was just such a man. If you see the movie or read the book, you will learn that after years of preparation and months of climbing, Mr. Miura, alone near the top of Mt. Everest, put on his skis and descended over 6,000 feet in less than two minutes. Then he fell. On film it appears that he will fall forever. The edge of a cliff rushes toward him, but he stops a few feet short of the edge. Did Yuichiro Miura succeed or did he fail? Of course, he succeeded. For me, the most poignant moment of the entire adventure comes on the eve of his attempt to be first to ski down Mt. Everest. He is alone near the top of the mountain. The wind is howling outside of his small tent. Six men have died while helping him reach this height. The price paid by everyone involved has been awesome. Yet, does Miura fear for his life? No. In his diary, he writes that his only fear is that of failing. He worries about letting everyone else down. This is a very powerful fear with which we are dealing. Fear of failure is a world class enterprise killer.

The only way I know to help you overcome your fear of failure is to tell you to work on it daily. Stare it in the eye and force it to retreat. Failure won't kill you in business. It can only slow you down. Don't close your eyes to the possibility of failure. Look at it. Examine it. What is it about failure that really bothers you? Discover the answer and never again hesitate because you might possibly fail. It is only when you close your eyes and refuse to face the possibility of failure that it can overcome you. Just like the child who told his father that he needed his stuffed dog to keep the monsters away:

"There are no monsters, son!"

"There are when I close my eyes, Daddy!"

So, don't go around with your eyes closed.

It is really worthwhile to witness a world class track and field competition. Nowhere else will you have an opportunity to see so many people of such great ability who are willing to face the possibility of defeat. Events such as

161

the pole vault and high jump amaze me, not just for the athletic ability demonstrated, but because in those events the athletes realize that every time they successfully complete a jump, the next one must be even higher - until they fail! Once they fail they are through for the day. Even the winners can fail on their last jumps as they try to push the bar up just a little higher. Are they really failing? Of course not. They have simply set their sights a little too high on that particular day. If you regard failing like a high jumper looks at it, you will never fail. Failing like this keeps you posted on whether or not your sights are set high enough.

Right now you may be at a crossroad. Should you really listen to the voices urging you to become an entrepreneur? Or should you continue to play it safe? You know the answer. If you continue in your indecision you will most certainly lose. Indecision is a greater enemy than an opposing army.

Here is a suggestion that you may want to follow. Write the following quotation out on a small card that you can carry with you in your pocket. Then read it often:

"Far better it is to dare mighty things, to win glorious triumphs, even though checkered by failure, than to take rank with those poor spirits who neither enjoy much nor suffer much because they live in the great twilight that knows neither victory nor defeat."
Theodore Roosevelt

PART FIVE SUMMARY

The Art of Becoming An Entrepreneur

1. Show your business plan only to friends, relatives, and neighbors whose help you need. Keep the rest of your acquaintances in the dark

2. Remember the two rules about working with government clerks, bureaucrats, and politicians:

> a. Focus on the issues and the facts. Pay no attention to the system or to the personalities

> b. Handle bureaucrats as you would handle children. Don't drop to their level, but try to bring them up to your level

3. The bottom, line on:

> a. Bankers - forget them. They will never be of any great help to the beginning entrepreneur

> b. Accountants - more helpful than bankers, but should be considered only in the manner you consider mechanics

> c. Lawyers - tell them what you intend to do and ask if, in their opinions, you will be violating any laws. Other than that, don't listen to a lawyer's opinion of the soundness of your project - and DON'T bring them in as partners!

4. The Competition: Welcome competitors. They are your best measure of how you are doing

5. Fear of Failure: *"Failure is only the opportunity to begin again, more intelligently."* (Henry Ford)

Part Six – The Final Touches

I Can Fly

August 3rd, 5:00 a.m.

I can hardly believe that it has been a year since my first balloon ride. This afternoon I will make a second attempt to take my flight test. A week ago I was prepared to fly with the FAA flight inspector, but a late afternoon thunderstorm forced us to cancel. The early forecast for today looks good. One year of worry, expense and frustration just for a short flight test. I have to wonder if it has been worthwhile.

I suspect that the greatest value this experience has provided is that I have actually completed the project. How often have I begun things, never to see them through! How easy it would have been for me to quit this one. I feel a much greater sense of accomplishment at having seen it through to the end than I do in finally being able to take passengers up in my balloon. Let's hope the weather holds this afternoon.

Overcoming All Obstacles

"The gods are well pleased when they see men contending with great adversities."
Seneca

165

I knew a man who said that solving problems was simple; you go through, over, under, or around them. Unfortunately, he always seemed to have a lot of problems. He was positive, energetic, and always seemed happy, yet he had more problems than anyone I've ever known. What do you think caused this? I think that the real source of my friend's problems was the manner in which he dealt with them. He looked at a problem as if it were a battle. With that attitude no wonder he was always in some sort of confrontation.

What, then, is the best way to handle problems? First of all, look at the facts. What is a problem? According to the dictionary a problem is simply "a question raised for inquiry, consideration, or solution." By keeping this definition in mind when faced with any sort of a problem, you will not only keep your sanity, you will also be in a proper frame of mind to solve it. You've got a problem? OK, then you have a question that has been raised for inquiry (answer it); a question raised for consideration (think about it); or a question raised for solution (solve it). Notice that nowhere in the definition of a problem does it say that you must worry about it! Yet what do most people do? Right. A lot of people spend more time worrying about their problems than they spend working them out.

The Duke of Wellington once said, "when one begins to turn in bed, it is time to turn out." That is some of the greatest advice an entrepreneur can receive. There will come times when you wake from a troubled sleep and begin worrying about the problems that will be facing you during the coming day. The best thing that you can do when that happens is to roll out of bed and begin working right then. The longer you lie awake worrying about your problems the bigger they will become. If you are going to be fatigued from lack of sleep anyway, why not lose sleep by working through the night instead of worrying through the night? You know as well as I do that most of the things we call problems are no more than uncertainties. And the only way I have found to deal with the anxiety that uncertainty brings is through faith and action.

I have faith that no matter what my problem, and no matter how it is resolved, the simple fact is that five hundred years from now it won't even be an interesting footnote on history - faith that if it is remembered one hundred years from now I am at least involved in something important - faith that if it is remembered ten years from now my company has at least survived - and faith in the fact that one year from now I will have totally forgotten that I had the problem in the first place. Let's face it, in the history of humankind few people have ever really had a 'world class' problem.

Action is the other solution to a problem. Remember, a problem is only a question raised for inquiry, consideration, or solution. The worst that can happen is that you may come up with a wrong solution. So? You are not going to find a perfect answer every time, but at least you have dealt with the problem and can now get on to other things. Whatever you do, don't lie awake worrying about your problems. Get up and do something about them.

No matter how great your problems seem to you, it is easy to find hundreds of people with far greater ones. Look around you and be glad that you don't have some of the other problems that are available. If you want to avoid high blood pressure then avoid mountain climbing over molehills. Sure you will have difficulties in getting your business going and even more in keeping it going. What did you expect? But difficulties aren't there to stop you. They are only there to be surmounted.

If you are now at the point of making the final commitment to start your own business then you should expect to feel a considerable amount of apprehension. I don't care what you may read about the founders of some of the greatest business concerns in America today, they all had this same kind of self-doubt. Yet they worked right through it. That is what you must do now. If you see a path before you with no obstacles you had better head in another direction because a clear path doesn't lead anywhere. Begin working out your plan now, TODAY. Go back and read the 'Summary' at the end of the first three sections of this book, and then begin laying the foundation for your new business. Begin with today's task and you will find that not only will you worry less about tomorrow, but that the ghosts you see as problems today will disappear in the sunlight of tomorrow. I firmly believe that you wouldn't have the desire to attain something unless you already had the capabilities necessary to succeed.

The way to work on the problems that face an entrepreneur at the beginning of a new venture is to begin with the attitude that 'I must do something.' Never approach a problem from the standpoint that 'Something must be done.' And by the way, that is the same way that problems must be handled once the business is up and rolling. YOU must do something. You are the entrepreneur, so answer it, think about it, or solve it. Then get on with your plan.

Don't think that the larger the problem the more time you must spend on it and the more involved the solution should be. Generally you will find that the simple solution is the best. At least it is the one you should consider first. It seems to me that one of the situations that exists today is that business people are valuing sophistication above common sense. What is wrong with simple solutions? Cut your problem down to the basic facts, write them down on a small piece of paper, and then use a little common sense. Solve it now! Quit wasting any more time in self-doubt, anxiety, and desperation. You can do anything you really want to do. Maybe not in the exact manner you first envision it, but if you get on with your plan you will be amazed at what you can achieve.

And yet, what do most men and women do? They come up with one excuse after another saying that the time is not yet right to put their idea in motion. I am reminded of the story of the farmer who asked his neighbor if he might borrow a rope. The neighbor said no because he was using the rope to tie up his milk. When the farmer pointed out that rope can't tie up milk, his neighbor replied, "I know, but when a man doesn't want to do something, one reason is as good as another." Haven't you been tying up your milk for long enough?

You don't need to be a genius in order to start your own business. All you need is energy, and a lot of it. Don't think that you have to solve every possible problem before you begin, either. It simply can't be done. A wise entrepreneur is the person who is aware of all that is going on and yet

169

knows what to overlook. Some things that appear as problems to your friends, neighbors, relatives, attorneys, and accountants just are not that important to the overall success of your plan. Remember, you are the only one with the vision to see the entire picture (otherwise someone else would be running your company), so don't become too involved with the problems, instead keep your eye on the goal.

I am not saying that you will be able to successfully solve every problem you encounter. Some will work out fine. Some will be handled incorrectly and thus create new problems. And some will simply go away. In fact, you will be surprised at how many of the smaller problems will disappear while you are working on the big ones. The ideal situation, of course, is to handle every problem the minute it arises, and to handle it perfectly. Unfortunately, the closer you get to the situation the less idealistic you can be. So don't worry about finding the 'perfect' answer to each and every problem. Just solve it and get on with life.

When you are faced with what seems to be a major problem, whether it arises before you open your doors, or when the business is booming, look for the answer within the problem. The seeds of solution are usually found somewhere in the problem itself. There is an excellent story about a king who owned a diamond that was scratched and no one could fix it. Eventually a man came along who etched a rose on the diamond and used the scratch for the stem. Why don't you build upon the scratches on your plan. The answers are already there if you look for them.

Actually, your solutions are really not that important in the long run. What is important is your persistence in getting on with the plan. Much of what you achieve in this life will come from persistence, and in business, persistence is the difference between winning and losing. When, you are at the beginning of a new venture you will find a particular set of problems that seem almost insurmountable: "Where will I get the money? How will I live while I'm starting out? Where will I find the people or the product I need? How will I tell my potential customers that I am in business?" Once the business is off and running, however, you will pick up new problems. But don't think that you should handle these new challenges any differently.

Throughout history there is example after example of persons who thought very wisely during quiet times and then acted foolishly when the pressure was on. Don't join the ranks of those poor souls who, when they are 'up to their asses in alligators,' forget that the objective is to drain the swamp. That old alligator cartoon makes one very important point, however. If your situation actually seems to be as hopeless as that of the 'swamp drainer' you should at least find some humor in it. Humor can often do more to help you with your problems than any other asset. Quit taking life and yourself so seriously, and your problems will be few.

If you set your mind to the fact that without any problems there wouldn't be any business either, a great weight will lift from your shoulders. No matter what your problem is at any particular point in your business, be assured that you will have even larger problems in the months and years ahead. Solve them and move on upstream. Keep on rowing and eventually you will reach your goal. Stop rowing (let the problems get to you) and you will quickly be washed downstream.

You should be grateful for your problems. As you overcome one and then another and then another, you become stronger and much better prepared to meet the next one. Feast on your difficulties and you will grow to reach heights of which you have not yet dreamed. In fact, you will find that each difficulty you face is much like a fine knife. As we grasp it by the blade or by the handle it will either cut us or serve us. Grab your biggest problem by the handle and answer it, think about it, or solve it as the situation requires. But whatever you do, make your problems serve you, they are the building blocks of business and of character.

When I was in my twenties I spent a great amount of time at sea, and it was there that I learned that there truly are no problems that cannot be overcome. In fact, I often irritate my associates when they come to me with a problem and I say, "Worse things happen at sea."

If you haven't tested your strength and courage against an ocean, you haven't yet fully experienced what it means to live. When taking your ship from one port to another, you had better hold to your course no matter what the conditions or you will never see land again. You may have to detour in a storm, but you had better not lose sight of your destination.

As an entrepreneur, you will find that guiding your business through the storms of free enterprise is much like being the captain of a great sailing ship. Your problems are the squalls and storms that blow, but without them you will never reach port, for a sailing ship cannot move in a dead calm. And you will be surprised to find that during times when the winds are fair and directly behind you, things don't go as well as when you are fighting the storm. For ships, like men, do poorly when the wind is directly behind, pushing them sloppily on their way. What you should pray for is a wind that is slightly opposed to your ship, for both people and ships do best when challenged. Sailing ships go nowhere in a calm, nor do kites reach for the sky without a stiff breeze, nor can you or your business flourish without some problems. Welcome them. Don't worry about them.

Far too many potentially successful businesses have failed because of an inordinate amount of time spent worrying about trifles. To succeed you must keep your eye on the principal objective and not let the little daily problems eat up all of your energy. Worry will cause fatigue faster than any other activity. And fatigue makes cowards of us all. How you handle your difficulties will show more about the type of person you are than any great success you may achieve. As the Chinese say, "The gem cannot be polished without friction, nor man perfected without trials."

Look forward to the trials that lie ahead. At least you will be able to say that you are alive and playing the game. Remember, if you are not tired and hurting you are merely a spectator. This new venture of yours may become the greatest game of your life. Look forward to it, to all of it, the good and the bad as well. It is going to be great fun.

There will come times when you will forget these words. There will be times when all seems lost, and you again begin to doubt yourself. Times when you feel like throwing in the towel. When you get to that point, what do you do? Obviously I can't answer that question with an absolute. There are times when it may be best to begin again, and there may be times when it may be best to forge ahead. But I can promise you that at those major turning points the best counsel is to always follow the boldest plan. When hopes seem smallest, be bold in your decisions and you will amaze even yourself with the results.

This may sound strange to you if you have never owned your own business, but you will be called upon quite often to exhibit a degree of bravery that you thought existed only on a battlefield. And I am speaking of bravery, not courage. For courage is only the hope that the terror is less than it appears. Bravery is much more, for it knows all the facts and the true extent of the danger faced. The greatest entrepreneurs, both men and women, are extremely bold and extremely brave. They know that victories that are easy are also cheap. They know that the only things worth having have come as the result of great struggles. They also know that there exists within every person worthy of the title entrepreneur, wells of thought and dynamos of energy, never suspected until emergencies arise. You are an entrepreneur, and within you is all the strength and character required to solve any problem, and to overcome any obstacle you face. You have decided to GO FOR IT. Nothing can stop you now.

As the years pass by, and as you meet crisis after crisis, a wonderful change will begin taking place in your life. No longer will you be haunted with self-doubt and anxiety. No longer will you lie awake worrying about tomorrows' problems. Instead you will grow into the person you knew, as a child, that you would one day become. The greater the difficulties you face, the stronger you will grow. Ask any great entrepreneur what were the most important events in their personal growth and, almost without exception, they will tell you about major problems that gave them new directions. Such people seem to almost look forward to adversity.

The great speaker, motivator, and educator, Cavett Robert once said that one of his most treasured possessions is a certain painting that his wife created. It has hung in his living room for years. Under the painting is printed the word, REVIRESCO. That word should be at the heart of every entrepreneur's creed. In short it means, "flourishing in adversity." You, too, will flourish in adversity. Sure you have some obstacles in your way right now. And, sure, you will have many more in the years ahead, but through it all remember, it doesn't matter what happens to you. All that matters is how you react to it. That is what makes the difference. You can do anything you set your mind to do. And you can overcome any obstacle in your way. What are you waiting for?

Your Attitude and How It Effects Others

"Nothing gives one person so much advantage over another as to remain always cool and unruffled under all circumstances."
Thomas Jefferson

Have you stopped to think, that now as you are beginning your own business, you are the top person in your business structure? Think about it for a minute. From now on there is no one else to turn to for the tough decisions. If you are depressed, that feeling will spread throughout your organization. If you are excited, then that feeling will spread throughout your organization. Until your company grows significantly, the mood of everyone involved, from the receptionist to the vice-presidents, will be a carbon copy of your mood. If you are worried about cash flow, the entire staff will feel financial pressure. And likewise, if you are confident about a significant increase in sales, you will find confidence throughout the company.

While it is true that no one's happiness but your own is in your power to achieve or to destroy, you must keep in mind that the overall 'happiness' of your company is a mirror image of your own attitude. This is, perhaps, a much greater responsibility than you now realize. When the storms arise, will your hand be steady on the helm? Or will you allow worry and despair to creep into the organization? At times, the responsibility of leadership can be awesome. But you are an entrepreneur, you wouldn't have been given the desire to begin your own business if you weren't capable of living up to the challenges. Just remember, however, that everyone in your company is looking up to you. To the outside world you must appear to be cut from granite. As a role model you may be inspiring future generations of entrepreneurs, and that in itself is a great responsibility.

There were times, in the past, when I did not live up to the demands of leadership, and showed my weakness to those who worked with me. Those were the moments that I am least proud of in all of my entrepreneurial activities. After all, whose idea was it to begin the business? It was the entrepreneur's idea, and it should be the entrepreneur's responsibility to live up to the demands of leadership. As Napoleon once said, "There is no greater immorality than to occupy a place you can't fill." Think about those words on a daily basis. Don't let your personal doubts and fears get so close to the surface that those around you become infected also. I'm not saying that there won't be times when, in the private recesses of your mind, you aren't concerned for the future of your business. What I am saying is that those are exactly the times when you are required to be brave.

You know as well as I do that people can't fake optimism. Therefore your optimistic attitude must be cultivated on a daily basis. Each morning you should read some short motivational statements. And at least once a week you should re-read your business plan. You may not have to read the entire plan every week, but you should at least read the sections that may contain answers to problems that are bothering you. Maybe you are falling a few months behind on your sales forecast. If so read that section of the plan and find out what may be going wrong. Did you simply over commit to a sales goal? Then revise the goal to a realistic amount and re-do your cash-flow analysis. Does that mean restructuring the company? Then do it. But quit carrying your worries on your shoulder where the rest of your employees can see them.

You must remember that in their own worlds, your employees are undergoing exactly the same trials and tribulations as you. Maybe they don't have to worry about keeping the company alive so that their jobs will be saved, but they have other financial and personal worries just as great from their perspectives. We all create our own little hells. Don't force yours on those who are working for you. You are the entrepreneur, and you can handle it. Do so with a smile on your face. Re-read the previous section about dealing with problems and get back to work. No entrepreneur has ever faced any 'world class' crisis. Those are for the politicians and generals to face. Entrepreneurs never have a real 'crisis.' They understand the meaning of the word as used by the Chinese. Their word for crisis combines the phrase 'dangerous wind' with the word 'opportunity.' And to an entrepreneur a crisis is welcome, for it is the source of opportunity.

It is really sad to see business people going around all day worrying, complaining, and generally making the lives of those around them miserable. I find that one of the most remarkable attributes of people is their predisposition to bring about and endure so much unnecessary anxiety. If you have a well-written business plan, there is no need for anxiety. So why force this unnatural pressure on others? Each day you should give yourself an attitude check and figure out how your attitude is affecting those around you. What part of your attitude is making your business grow and what elements of your attitude are spreading gloom and doom throughout the company?

I am not saying that you should be complacent about poor sales, weak cash flow, and other problems. What I am saying is that, for the most part, those are problems that are for you, the entrepreneur, to solve. Don't pass them on to your employees unless you also give those employees the authority to solve the problems. Of course you are going to have your anxious moments, but only tolerate productive anxiety within yourself. Make tension work for you, and keep a smile on your face and in your voice. You will be amazed at the effect it will have on those around you. Is that going to be difficult at times? Yes. But you are the entrepreneur. You started all of this. Now get on with your business.

Too many new entrepreneurs seem to think that once they have secured the initial capital with which to begin their businesses the rest will be easy. A little reflection will reveal how foolish that idea really is. Nothing in life worth having is easy to acquire or achieve. So what? You must have perseverance and confidence in yourself. You must truly believe that you were meant to begin this business and that you have the capacity to make a success of it. It may cost you a great deal of anxiety and suffering, but what of that? Whatever the cost you must go on. You are an entrepreneur. Keep faith in yourself and in the principles set out in this book. You will be tested on your faith, and you pass the test only if you keep a level head and a cheery disposition at the time of your greatest need. Quit worrying and keep working.

The manner in which you approach the daily problems of your business will be mirrored by each and every person who works for you. When everything is looking the worst you must show more bravery than you now think you have. Bravery, in fact, is the greatest asset of anyone in authority. If you show it, so will those around you. And a group of brave people cannot be stopped. You don't have to be without concern in order to be happy in business. The happiest people I know have an enormous number of things that concern them. But they have learned the art of coping with them in a positive manner. Don't try to appear important by letting everyone around you share your concerns. You are the leader. Get out front and lead!

If you once begin to share your problems, and your worries, with the people around you, the end of your days as an entrepreneur are in sight. I'm not saying that you have to solve every problem alone. However, if an employee or other associate isn't responsible for solving the particular problem that concerns you, then don't load your worry on their shoulders. Think of yourself as a pillar of strength, inner strength. The story is told of an old lady, bent with arthritis, loaded down with a heavy grocery bag, who was waiting for a bus. A kindly man offered to help her with her load. She smiled and said, "No thanks. If I want help today, I'll *need* it tomorrow." Take a lesson from that lady. If you want someone to share your burdens today, you will need their help tomorrow.

One of the most common causes for the failure of a business is the loss of confidence by its founder. And the fastest road to a loss of confidence is by sharing your concerns with people who are not in a position to solve your problems. As an entrepreneur you must be willing to suffer in silence. The success of your business may well depend upon it. A positive, cheerful attitude will do more to insure success than all the money and all the knowledge in the world.

Just What Is Success?

"Business was originated to produce happiness, not to pile up millions."
B. C. Forbes

If you are to become not only a successful entrepreneur, but also a happy one in the years to come, it is important that you spend a moment or so reflecting on what success actually means to you. Is it a large bank account (how large?), a new house (how new?, how big?), a fast car (how fast?), or retirement (what will you do then?). As you think about these trappings of success you may realize that none of them are all that essential - and, thus, none are truly measures of your success. How then do you measure success?

My favorite description of success is that it is a journey, not a destination. And it is what *you* become along the way that tells whether or not you are a success. To me, success consists of having the courage, endurance, and the will to follow through with the task you have begun. It is the ability to concentrate all of your energy on today's tasks and accomplish them to the very best of your ability. Once you are able to go to bed every night with the feeling that you have given your very best effort that day, whether or not you completed all that you set out to do, then you are a success. This is not the destination. It is only a resting point on your way to the next destination. It is while you are traveling along the way that you discover you are successful.

Unfortunately, too many of us have become conditioned to

thinking of success only in monetary terms. If you are dreaming of mountains of money, you will never achieve the sense of security that a personal reserve of knowledge, experience, and ability brings to the successful entrepreneur. The successful entrepreneur may go broke a time or two, but he or she becomes stronger at the end of each day of accomplishment. Be happy with who you are and with what you have. Quit looking around to see what everyone else has. When money alone is your goal, you can no longer appreciate the things that you have already acquired. Instead, you make yourself miserable by wishing for what the other fellow possesses. A happy, successful entrepreneur is a person who can be contented with little, yet he or she is one who always wants and works for more. By being contented with only a few personal possessions, you will find yourself among the wealthiest of all individuals. Appreciate what you already have. Then you can begin to look for more.

What is success? Success is the ability to live your life in your own way. Follow your own game plan – not someone else's. If you reach, for goals that you have set for yourself, and if you achieve those goals, then you will be a success by anyone's standards.

Years ago, I measured my success in ways that the outside world could also see. I thought that my own swimming pool would be one item that would tag me as a success. I could take an early morning swim, have breakfast, and then go my successful way to work. Eventually I was able to purchase a house with a pool. I anxiously awaited warmer weather - the water had to be warm enough for a swim. All right! Warm weather arrived. For the next six weeks I woke up each morning burdened by the thought of a cool swim before breakfast. Then, fortunately, I thought about how much nicer another thirty minutes of sleep would be. I love to sleep as late as possible. Finally I forced myself out of bed three mornings in a row, had a swim before breakfast, and hated everything having to do with early morning swimming. I swam around and around the pool thinking how much more I'd enjoy that extra thirty minute pre-breakfast nap than waddling around in all of that cold water!

What does this have to do with success? Everything. Until that summer I had viewed success as the acquisition of material things. My friends were successful. They had pools. I wanted one, too. Those disliked early morning swims started me thinking about what success really means, and, suddenly, I realized that I had become a success long before I could afford the pool. The pool was only a way for me to show off my success to the outside world. It really didn't have anything else to do with success. It was then that I learned that real success doesn't come from ease or riches, or even from the praise of others. It comes from doing something worthwhile and doing it well. Real success isn't what you get from your work, it is what you become as a result of it.

In the process of becoming an entrepreneur you will experience despair, frustration, anxiety, and at times, anger. You will be asked (and will ask yourself) to make many sacrifices for the sake of your business. In the end, you may wind up with a great deal of money. However, long before you acquire wealth of any note you will already have become a great success. No doubt, you will have made many mistakes along the way, but you will be amazed at how many mistakes your success will cover up. Enjoy the journey and you will be a success from its start.

One key to maintaining a feeling of success as you progress is to quit judging your progress by comparing yourself to others.

There is a story of the father who was trying to motivate his son to study. He said to his son, "When Abraham Lincoln was your age he walked ten miles to school and then he studied at night by firelight." The son replied, "That's a good story, Pop, but when Lincoln was your age he was the president of the United States."

Comparisons have a way of backfiring, don't they?

When is it that you will become a success? That is up to you. If you have been following the steps given in this book, you have already begun to be successful. Are your ideas written out on paper? Have you begun to refine your choices? Is your business plan available in writing for you to review? If you have not already taken those steps, now is the time to do so. Money is never successful. People are! You are! Many little triumphs equal one big success. As Henry Wadsworth Longfellow wrote:

> "The heights by great men reached and kept
> Were not attained by sudden flight,
> But they, while their companions slept,
> Were toiling upward in the night."

Successful people are the ones who climb ever higher. The various levels of economic achievement are not meant to be stopping points any more than the rung of a ladder is meant to be a place on which to stand forever. Both are there to let you know that you can go even higher. Practice your success. You will become better at it - and you will not see it deserting you.

For your life as an entrepreneur to be one of happiness, you must spend a few minutes of each and every day thinking about what success really means to you. Money, influence, and power are only passing things. Your life can be considered to be a success if you gain the ability to be aware of who and what you are. You must take time, each day, to stop, think, and enjoy your progress. Don't waste time wishing for things you don't have - instead, rejoice in your accomplishments, in the things you do have, and in your looking forward to the progress you will make tomorrow.

Once you get ahead, it is important that you protect your lead, just as in baseball, by increasing it. If you have been, hitting doubles, now you must strive to hit triples and home runs. Be the best you possibly can be. Be dissatisfied with your progress. Be discontented! Those two negatives are the bases of most positive advances. Don't fall into the trap of believing that you "have it made". Prosperity and ease have their own ways of testing you. You are already a success. Feel it - deep in your bones. Success is an ongoing process.

Charles Evans Hughes, justice of the supreme court, put it this way:

"One of the most important lessons in life is that success must continually be won and is never finally achieved. Every day is one of test. Every day puts at risk all that has

been gained. The greater the apparent achievement, the more serious is the risk of loss. The further you have climbed, the more disastrous the fall. As has well been said, it is not worthwhile to talk of the end of a period, for you are always at the beginning of a new one. You cannot rest content."

Knowing When To Quit

"Be like the bird, who, halting in his flight on limb too slight, yet sings - knowing he has wings."
Victor Hugo

Knowing when to quit may be a strange title for a section in a book about going into business on your own, but it is a topic that must be covered. There are two major signals that tell you when it is time to quit. I know this to be so. The two times I ignored those major signals, I received some extra pain that could have been avoided. The first of these two signals is boredom - and the second signal is any positive evidence that comes along to tell you that the business is going to fail.

Right now, as you are in the formative stages of your new business, it likely does not seem possible to you that you might become bored with your business. Well, you really can! Often, people stay enthused during the time when the challenge is high - when the going is really rough. As soon as things smooth out, boredom may set in. If you find this happening to you, it is important that you turn the day-to-day operation of your business over to others so that you might move on to different things - hopefully things that are bigger and better.

Empires are built by young-acting people. Empires are lost by old-acting people. Boredom, no matter what your age may be, tends to make you act old, tired, and dull. Beware if this is what is happening to you. If what you are doing bores you, you will rapidly become soft, dull, tired, and old-acting, and your business will be in real trouble.

You will have to decide if your business is truly in trouble - or is it that you are tired and bored? Is there finally no longer any hope that the business can survive financially? Or is the answer to that question clouded because of your fatigue and boredom? Here is where you walk that razor's edge of personal conflict. The dilemma is a terrible one. It is a dilemma that most entrepreneurs have to face time and time again.

Do you recall the definition of entrepreneur? An entrepreneur is one who is willing to accept the risk of loss for the potential of gain. There is a Japanese proverb that says, "Where profit is, loss is hidden nearby."

How true that is! Often, however, the fact that the business is steadily going downhill is hidden by one's sense of duty. How can you see through the dreams, the hopes, and the sense of duty to know what is really happening? What do you do about it if things are going badly?

The best guide you have to the true state of affairs of your business is your written business plan. It can help you tell whether the business is going out of control or if you are just weary. Businesses don't turn sour overnight. If you refer to your business plan at least once a week, over the course of a year it will become painfully obvious that your business is falling apart - or it may become joyfully apparent that your business is doing just fine, but that you need a rest. Should your business be a month or two behind the planned schedule, it is likely that you are experiencing a personal low. To overcome such a low, listen to motivational tapes, read some good books, get around interesting people, relax, and go forward. If, however, your business is really in trouble, don't make the mistake made by so many other entrepreneurs - don't simply keep on working long after all hope is gone. Don't ride your business down to the ground. If the business is going to crash for certain, it is a wise entrepreneur who jumps before it hits.

I have ridden a business all the way down to the ground. That almost cost me the will to begin again. You should think of it this way. Without at least a little altitude, your parachute cannot possibly open. If you wait until you can almost reach down and touch the ground, you may not survive the fall. Now, don't misunderstand me. When I suggest that you jump, I am not advising that you walk away from business problems and leave them to someone else. As the captain of your own ship, you should be the last one to leave. Yes, there may come a time when you have to face the fact that things haven't worked out the way you planned them, and that the best thing to be done is to shut down the operation and begin again. Surely that will be painful. It takes a great deal more courage to quit than it does to keep on struggling in a losing cause.

When to quit is a hard, hard lesson to learn. When I was growing up, folks taught me that a person should be slow to undertake a task, but once the task was undertaken to go through with it. To me that meant that, no matter what, I must make my business succeed. I believed in that line from the movie, "Rocky" which went, "Maybe I can't win, but I'm going to go the distance."

I misunderstood what "going the distance" meant. "Going the distance" means that once you have committed yourself to a project you must give it your very best shot. Hold nothing back. Become the best you possibly can, and do the best you possibly can do. Follow your dreams of building a better world through building more and better businesses. Failures will be out there waiting for you. Don't you fail with them!

Let me remind you that the title of this book is "The Art of Becoming an Entrepreneur," not "How to Start a Business." It is much easier to open a business than it is to become an entrepreneur. To succeed in becoming an entrepreneur you must dedicate yourself to a way of life, not just to a particular business or to a certain plan. You have to really *dedicate* yourself to this pursuit, for it is only true dedication that will enable you to carry out your plans long after the beginning enthusiasm is gone. You may have to close a business or two, but if you are truly dedicated to becoming an entrepreneur, you will hang on as long as you can, decide to close the doors, and then you will begin again. You need not worry about what may happen to your reputation should you fail at your business. People know that you aren't responsible for everything that happens to you - but you are responsible for the way you respond to the circumstances in which you find yourself. Your prayer should be, "Let me win, and if I cannot win, let me be brave in the attempt."

Difficult it is to make that final decision to close a business into which you and others have poured your hearts and souls. In the end, however, it is only you who can make the decision; the last few paces you must walk alone. Although there are different types of advice you might seek before you act to close your business, I firmly believe that by the time you get around to asking for advice, you have cast the die. My personal advice is that you contemplate the situation in peace and tranquility - and that you make the decision on your own. You decided to begin the business. You should decide to close it if that is what is necessary. Such a decision relates to your current business. The decision to close that business is not a decision to end your entrepreneurial career.

Experience is the name everyone gives to their mistakes. As you go on to begin another business, try to remember your "experiences" with the one that failed. Draw strength from those mistakes. Profit from them. Recover from them.

Sometimes I feel that the only things I ever learned from experience were the things I really didn't want to know. Knowledge, however, is always useful. For example, Thomas Edison spent a lot of time and effort in a search for a new source of natural rubber. His discouraged assistant reported that they had made 50,000 experiments, but, still, there were no positive results. Edison replied, "Results! We have wonderful results! We now know which 50,000 things won't work!"

Edison, like the rainmakers of the old West, knew that the rain would come if he just beat on the drum long enough.

Yes, it is no fun to admit defeat, but if defeat comes to you, don't let it destroy you. The ups and downs are all part of the entrepreneur's territory. Like sunshine versus rain, defeat and victory are not enemies. They are simply facts of life that you must accept. If one venture fails, use the experience to gain a better perspective, to prepare for bigger ventures. Remember Abraham Lincoln's words, "I shall prepare myself and my opportunity *must* come ."

Getting angry helps sometimes, too. After Davy Crockett lost an election in Tennessee, he gave a farewell speech. Here is what he said: "You can go to hell. I'm going to Texas!"

Move to another town or another state if that is what it takes. Or go to Texas (a real state of mind!) But whatever you do, get going again.

You have to be able to shrug if the need ever arises. There is always the chance that your venture might fail. Face that prospect from the start, and don't let it destroy you should it happen. Only when you fail will you know that you truly reached to your limit. Failure is simply a sign that you attempted to surpass yourself. Here is what B. C. Forbes had to say about failing in business:

> *"History has demonstrated that the most notable winners usually encountered heartbreaking obstacles before they triumphed. They finally won because they refused to become discouraged by their defeats."*

Suffering is not that important relative to what it is you are trying to accomplish, so don't let suffering scar you permanently. Keep your faith. Press forward with your face to the light. The only time you must not fail is the last time you try.

Business Is Booming, Now What?

"Immortality is a momentary thing."
M. S. Forbes

The previous section covered the possibility of a business failure. There is yet one more obstacle that an entrepreneur must overcome - the possibility of fantastic success! How you handle success will separate you from the ordinary business person and allow you to claim the title, entrepreneur.

Just as a business failure doesn't end the career of an entrepreneur, neither should success. The failure or success of a business should be no more than another milestone in your life. It is important, therefore, that you do not wait until a particular business comes to either full success or full failure before you make plans to begin another business. Possibly, your next business will be a division or subsidiary of the original business - or it may be a completely new and different business. No matter which type of new business it may be, don't wait until what you are currently doing is at a tidy end point before you start the wheels in motion toward building something new.

How do you know if it is time to begin something new?

One obvious signal is that you find yourself beginning to slack off a little. When you begin to arrive at work later and leave work earlier, you begin to lose a lot of the value you have to your own business. Someone with more enthusiasm would probably do a better job if you would let that person take your place. If the business is running smoothly and making a profit you should try to find your own replacement. Finding your replacement will allow you to remain creative, to keep you from becoming bored. Success is not a resting place. It is a continual journey that should take you an entire lifetime to complete.

As you might suspect, there is a very thin line between walking away from problems and going on to bigger things. Even businesses that are growing and making profits have serious problems - sometimes many times each day. So, before you move on to bigger and better things, carefully evaluate your business to ensure that it is well-grounded enough to survive without your constant personal touch. If all is well, you should take the advice of Will Rogers who said, "Even if you're on the right track you'll get run over if you just sit there."

The great American entrepreneurs seldom simply retired from business to enjoy their wealth in quiet and comfort. They continued to build throughout their lives. Humans were intended to work, but not necessarily at a "job". We work because we like to work. Certainly, you should have things to do and to enjoy outside of work, but do enjoy your work.

Wouldn't it be sad if you were to miss all of those wonderful moments in life that exist outside of your business? People don't remember the days that pass by, they remember the moments that have meaning. If you let too many of those special moments with friends, lovers, and family pass you by, you will have let life itself pass you by. Don't discover at your life's end that you have never really lived. Entrepreneurs tend to be egocentric, and so it is somewhat difficult for many of them to realize that they are no more than minor characters in every biography other than their own! Play a larger role in a few other biographies. Expand your social contacts outside of the range of your business interests. Not only is this fun to do, it is these outside contacts that generally plant the seeds of still greater ventures on which you can embark.

Be careful to not let your ego become inflated by your success, however. No matter how large your business becomes, and no matter how high you rise in the public eye, keep in mind that there will always be millions of people who have never heard of you for every one who knows your name. As Marcus Aurelius once said:

> *"Consider how many do not even know your name, and how many will soon forget it, and how those who now praise you will presently blame you."*

All right! You have built a great business. Now what? You need to consider what it is that you are going to do with the rest of your life. If you are fortunate enough to have built a company that can run for a time in your absence, and if you have earned enough money to be able to afford a few luxuries, why not take a brief rest from it all. Travel. Make new friends. Explore new frontiers of your mind - or of the world. Try new experiences. If you enjoy them, you may decide to repeat them, but if you put these things off, you may never be able to approach them again. Your life is not endless on this planet, nor are the lives of those you love. You have to live while you are yet alive!

Thinking only of your business and dwelling on your good fortune to "have it made" will quickly cause you to fall into a rut and to be only inches away from becoming a has-been. During the time you are building your business you will, of necessity, concentrate on accumulating material things and pursuing material goals. In the process of doing so, don't forget that happiness comes from within, from what you are - not from what you have. Granted, it is difficult to decide each day whether to devote your energy toward improving the world or toward enjoying it. So therefore try to do both. Balance your life between work and play right from the start. Without work life quickly becomes grim, and with no play, life goes sour.

Don't try to justify a life of all work and no play by saying that you are doing it for your family. It is a big mistake to believe that you are working for others. It is human nature to put work first - and you are not possessed of a warped personality because you enjoy your work more than you enjoy other things. You do, however, owe it to yourself to expand your life beyond its current boundaries. Take up new hobbies, listen to different music, read different types of books, make friends outside of your regular range of contacts - in other words, strive to expand your life. After several years, when your business is well grounded, take several months off to begin dreaming again. You have more than just one idea to pass on to this world.

Your prayers will all be answered, not when you get that for which you asked, but when you become that which you know you can be. Just as you must not worry over failure, don't worry about success. Success should not change you, it should only make you more of what you are already. What you are, at long last, is an entrepreneur!

Part Six Summary

1. Definition of a problem: a question raised for inquiry, consideration, or solution. Solve the problem. Don't worry about it.

2. Your attitude will constantly be reflected by your employees. A B P (Always Be Positive!)

3. The key to becoming a success is to remember that success is a journey, not a destination.

4. If your plan doesn't work out, remember: The business plan failed. You did not fail at becoming an entrepreneur.

5. Once the business is a success, ask yourself this question: "Am I truly an entrepreneur, or am I only a business person?"

Epilogue

August 3rd, midnight:

Well, I did it! I am now a licensed hot air balloon pilot. Now what? For starters, I will be entering my first balloon race later this month - and another one in September. I am going to try to sharpen up my piloting skills enough to place high in one of those events. Then what? Obviously, I'll go ahead and get my commercial rating, but that doesn't appear to be a big deal. Perhaps I should look into gas ballooning? Maybe try for some new balloon flying records. Also, there must be a way to make some money ballooning! In fact, I believe that I have an exciting idea for doing just that. Time to begin a new plan!

Dreams and Duties

"A dream comes true only if you believe in it."
Lorenzo Hagerty

Well, here you are at the end of another book. How many books have you now read about going into business? One? Three? Seven? More? It doesn't matter. You don't have to read any more books in order to get started. In fact, if you followed the instructions in the first three parts, you should already be well on your way to opening your new business. If you haven't yet taken any of the steps outlined in those first three parts, then you must ask yourself the question, "Why didn't I?" You certainly have the imagination and thinking power required - otherwise you would not have read this book. How about the courage, the drive, and the determination it takes? Do you have them also? Well, you almost certainly do, for without them you would not have read this entire book as eagerly as you did. All that is left for you to do is to decide to carry through with your idea. Why not make that decision today?

It is that simple. You have your dream. Now you can use your decision to hold your dream in front of you and set your eyes firmly on the goal it represents. One day, while driving along an expressway, I saw a very large piece of paper blowing across the road. As the cars ahead sped by, the paper was drawn into their vortexes and into the paths of the cars following. It was obvious that an accident was likely to happen should the paper land on someone's windshield. There was no way to pull off the roadway or to stop without creating an accident myself, so I drove on. Lucky for me, the paper didn't land on my windshield. Rather, it blew along the side of my car, and I continued on my way. For an instant I was tempted to look back to see what became of the cars following me, but I immediately realized how dangerous it would be to look back while going forward at fifty miles an hour. Just as that thought crossed my mind, the driver in front of me applied his brakes and I was barely able to stop without my car hitting his. Had I been looking backward, I would probably not be writing this now.

The art of being an entrepreneur is much like the art of driving at highway speeds. If you take your eyes away from where you are heading, even for only an instant, you may wind up as a statistical note that reads: "One more entrepreneur-to-be who couldn't concentrate on the task of getting started."

So, give up a little of your free time and begin working on your project today.

Look to the future. Place your hopes and dreams in the future. Then, do the work today that will move you in that direction. Don't yearn for the future - work for it. It will arrive quickly. Place your hopes and plans in more than one possibility. As an entrepreneur, it is your responsibility to consider everything, to keep your alternative lines of action open. Plan your future. Then begin working on your plan.

No matter what you think your abilities to be right now, there is one fact about them that will not change: your past will not determine your future unless you permit it to. No matter your experience, your bank balance, your education, or your age, it is never out of place to begin! Picture for yourself Benjamin Franklin in his eighties adding larger bed chambers and a big library to his house - a time in life when most people might be thinking of getting something a little smaller. When asked about this disparity between Franklin's ways of doing things and the ways of other people his age, Franklin noted, "It has always been my maxim to live as if I were to live always."

Franklin's philosophy is a good one for you to adopt as you begin today on your new adventure. What is there to lose? In the great scheme of the universe, what, really, do you have to lose by making a serious attempt at becoming an entrepreneur?

As many, many people before you have found out, there is no security in working for others. You might prefer to grasp the real security that comes from employing yourself. Only then are you likely to use your natural abilities to their fullest. That is real security. Now is the time for you to work on the plans and dreams that set you apart from the crowd.

When I think of you, about to begin on a new adventure in life, I am reminded of an experience I had one Friday night as I was returning home from a business trip. Our plane had just taken off into a cold, dark, rainy sky, when suddenly we broke through the cloud cover and into the clear, unlimited sky above. I looked out the window and, off to our left, was the moon, just beginning its rise over the eastern horizon. The moon appeared to be twice its normal size, and it was a brilliant white color. What really impressed me, however, was that our plane appeared to actually be higher than the moon. It was as if we had broken the grasp of gravity and had soared into the heavens. What a magnificent feeling that was!

Once you begin your own flight to success, you too, will experience such a feeling. There is simply nothing quite like being in charge of your own future. You will have to live with the failures, but they are more than compensated for by successes. The fact that you have read this book is evidence that you have a calling to become an entrepreneur. Not only is that one of the higher callings of humankind, it is a calling of critical importance to the world today. There are massive changes underway in the world's social structure. In the United States this change began in the 1960's. Now the changes are maturing into a call for improvement in human society - a crescendo of calling that will carry us into the future. How well we live up to the responsibility of living in these interesting times may well determine the quality of life on earth for centuries to come. Seldom in history has a generation had such a chance to move our species ahead or behind so quickly. You are indeed at the right place at the right time.

Appendix - Business Plan Outline

The following simple outline is explained in detail in Part Three.

BUSINESS PLAN OF XYZ CORPORATION

A. GUIDANCE STATEMENT

    1. Mission

    2. Goals

    3. Objectives

    4. Strategies

B. SPECIFIC OBJECTIVES

    1. Specific Corporate Goals

    2. Executive Objectives

    3. Marketing Objectives

    4. Sales Objectives

    5. Product Development Objectives

C. MARKETING STRATEGY

    1. Target Market

    2. Geographic Distribution

    3, Sales Aids and Training

D. INCOME AND CASH FLOW PROJECTIONS

E. MANPOWER

F. INTERNAL OPERATIONS

G. FINANCIAL STATEMENTS

The Art of Becoming An Entrepreneur